THE **TOP 100**
JUICES

THE TOP 100
JUICES

SARAH OWEN

DUNCAN BAIRD PUBLISHERS

LONDON

THE TOP 100 JUICES Sarah Owen

Distributed in the USA and Canada by Sterling Publishing Co., Inc.
387 Park Avenue South, New York, NY 10016-8810

This edition first published in the UK and USA in 2007 by Duncan Baird Publishers Ltd
Sixth Floor, Castle House, 75–76 Wells Street, London W1T 3QH

Managing Editor: Grace Cheetham
Editor: Ingrid Court-Jones
Managing Designer: Suzanne Tuhrim
Commissioned photography: Toby Scott at Simon Smith studios
Styling: Mari Mererid Williams

Library of Congress Cataloging-in-Publication Data Available
ISBN: 978-1-84483-494-5

10 9 8 7

Typeset in Helvetica Condensed
Color reproduction by Colourscan, Singapore
Printed in China for Imago

For information about custom editions, special sales, premium and corporate purchases, please
contact Sterling Special Sales Department at 800-805-5489 or specialsales@sterlingpub.com.

Publisher's Note: The information in this book is not intended as a substitute for professional
medical advice and treatment. If you are pregnant or breastfeeding or have any special dietary
requirements, allergies, or medical conditions, it is recommended that you consult a medical
professional before following any of the information or recipes contained in this book. Duncan
Baird Publishers, or any other persons who have been involved in working on this publication,
cannot accept responsibility for any errors or omissions, inadvertent or not, that may be found
in the recipes or text, nor for any problems that may arise as a result of preparing one of these
recipes or following the advice contained in this work.

Notes on the recipes
Unless otherwise stated:
• Use fresh herbs
• 1 tsp = 5ml, 1 tbsp = 15ml, 1 cup = 225ml

CONTENTS

KEY TO SYMBOLS

 dairy-free

 nut-free and seed-free

 citrus-free

 fat-free

 low-calorie

 low-kilojoule

 low-GI (less than 55)

 low-GL (less than 10)

beauty plus

introduction

There are a number of reasons why juicing is so popular in the twenty-first century. Top of the list is that fresh juices and smoothies are seriously delicious, especially as you can tweak each recipe to suit your own taste. Plus, freshly prepared juices are bursting with health-boosting vitamins, minerals, antioxidants, trace elements, and plant nutrients to make you feel great and look fabulous. Drinking them is a fast-track way to get the recommended two to five cups of fruit and vegetables a day. Homemade juices are also guaranteed to be free from health-depleting additives, preservatives, artificial flavorings and colorings.

EXTRA HEALTH BENEFITS

Processed soft drinks often contain 90 percent water, a huge hit of sugar and/or sweeteners and chemicals to add flavor. "Pure" juices are frequently reconstituted concentrates that have been heat-treated to prolong shelf life, which means they provide very few nutrients. Even "freshly squeezed" juices have been kept on the shelf for several hours, if not days, and they are less nutritionally valuable than freshly-prepared juices because many vitamins lose potency when exposed to light, heat, and air. Only freshly made juices retain the highest level of nutrients, which the body can digest readily. Raw juices drunk on an empty stomach are absorbed into the bloodstream within 15 minutes.

Fresh juices are also abundant in enzymes responsible for the digestion and absorption of food into the body, insuring optimal metabolism and high energy levels. Cooking fruit and vegetables destroys these enzymes, whereas juicing releases them and allows the body to utilize them easily. Another important health benefit is that juices and smoothies are generally low in fat and many are completely fat free.

BEAUTY BENEFITS

It is true that much of beauty comes from within, so it's as important to cleanse the inside of your body as it is the outside. Many of the nutrients found in fruit and vegetables help rid the body of toxins, which, in turn, leads to clearer, brighter skin, and fewer pimples. Getting a nutrient-rich diet from regularly drinking juices will also give you healthy hair and nails, naturally, without you having to spend lots of money on beauty products. Stress, ill-health, and lack of sleep will eventually take their toll on appearance, and that's why juices that banish stress and boost immunity are so beneficial. Finally, you can watch the pounds disappear if you opt for low-calorie, fat-burning juices—and they taste delicious, too!

WHICH JUICE?

Smoothies are particularly filling and make a good breakfast option. Children tend to like sweeter, fruit-based juices and banana-based smoothies. Convalescents often cope better with half a glass of juice at a time.

All fresh juices boost general health, but each recipe also has specific therapeutic benefits depending on the nutrients present in the ingredients. The recipes are divided into eight chapters, each with a different focus. Detoxifiers help to flush energy-sapping toxins out of the body and are best drunk on an empty stomach. Weight Shifters are low in fat and calories and, in some cases, help the body to burn fat. Energy Boosters revive energy slumps at any time and are rich in fatigue-fighting nutrients. Stress Busters contain ingredients known for their calming properties, and make good bedtime options. Antiagers are rich in antioxidants and phytochemicals that protect the skin against free-radical damage and minimize wrinkles. Digestion Soothers relieve many digestive complaints and are suitable for those with sensitive stomachs. Immunity Strengtheners contain vitamins, minerals, antioxidants, and phytochemicals to help boost the body's ability to destroy free radicals, viruses, bacteria, and cancer cells. The last chapter, Brain Boosters and Mood Enhancers, is packed with ingredients that balance the chemistry of the brain and improve memory and concentration levels.

WHICH JUICER?

There are many different juicers available, but it all comes down to a basic choice between a centrifugal juicer or a masticating machine. Of the two, a centrifugal juicer is the less expensive option—it spins the fruit or vegetable around on a serrated blade, straining the juice through a filter. The pulp is either retained inside the machine or ejected into a separate container. A masticating juicer is usually a larger, heavier piece of equipment, which crushes the ingredients between rollers and pushes them through a wire mesh, extracting more juice than a centrifugal juicer and leaving a drier pulp. A juicer with a spout is a good option, because juicing directly into a glass rather than into a jug means less dishwashing. For smoothies, you will need a blender that whizes the ingredients with a rotating blade in a plastic or glass jug.

STORE FOR MAXIMUM FRESHNESS

The nutritional value of most fruit and vegetables tends to deteriorate over time, so don't store ingredients for too long before juicing them, although refrigerating or freezing them helps to retain more of the nutrients. The exceptions are citrus fruits, and bananas, which need to be kept at room temperature and used when their skins turn yellow. Avocados ripen at room temperature, after which they should be used immediately or kept in the refrigerator. Store nuts and seeds in an airtight container in a dry, dark place.

IT'S ALL IN THE PREPARATION

Wash fruit and vegetables under running water immediately before use, scrubbing away any dirt on root vegetables with a bristle brush. If the produce is organic, a quick rinse will do. Some ingredients, such as avocado, pineapple, mango, papaya, melon, orange, lemon, lime, banana, squash, and yam, need to be peeled. Many others, such as apple, apricot, pear, plum, peach, and cucumber, can be juiced with their skins on. In each recipe, the list of ingredients will tell you when a fruit or vegetable needs to be peeled, except for carrots, which depend on their source: non-organic carrots need peeling.

To prevent soft fruit, such as peaches and plums, becoming mushy and clogging up the blade, alternate them with firmer fruit. Insure you properly juice leafy ingredients, such as spinach and watercress, by wrapping each leaf around a chunk of fruit or vegetable. If the left-over pulp seems particularly wet, re-juice it to extract more liquid. Once all the ingredients have been put through the juicer, stir the juice well to mix them. Sprinkle any nuts or seeds over and drink immediately to gain maximum benefits.

After each use, clean the juicer thoroughly in warm, soapy water (very hot water can warp the plastic). The best way to remove fruit and vegetable stains from the white plastic parts of the juicer is by soaking them first and then scrubbing them with a solution made up of one part white vinegar to two parts water.

USEFUL INFORMATION

- Each recipe makes approximately enough juice for two servings, although quantities vary depending on the size, ripeness, and juiciness of your individual ingredients.

- Don't be tempted to juice bruised or blemished fruit and vegetables, as they won't taste good and will lack nutrients. Choose high-quality, organic produce for optimum health benefits.

- Some people find that when they start drinking freshly prepared juices regularly, they tend to urinate more frequently, and experience a slight headache. This is owing to the diuretic effect of the concentrated juices, and toxins leaving the body. Don't worry—this is perfectly normal. Simply drink lots of water to help flush out any toxins. After a couple of days, your body will get used to the detoxifying effects of the juices and these symptoms will fade.

apple, lemon & lime

NUTRIENTS
Vitamins C, K, beta-carotene, folate; calcium, magnesium, phosphorus, potassium; bioflavonoids; limonin; malic acid; pectin

For maximum cleansing, drink this tangy juice on an empty stomach first thing in the morning.

Apples are detoxifying largely because they contain pectin, a type of soluble fiber, which helps to flush out cholesterol, toxins, and heavy metals from the body through the liver and kidneys. The citric acid in the lemon and lime also helps to eliminate waste. Lemon stimulates the digestive juices and has a slightly laxative effect. Always keep lemons and limes for juicing at room temperature, as they produce more juice when they are warm.

Give this juice an extra citrus kick by finely grating a little lemon and lime zest on top.

RECIPE

4 apples, cut into wedges
1 lemon, peeled and
    quartered
2 limes, peeled and quartered

Press alternate chunks of fruit through a juicer. Stir and drink immediately.

cantaloupe melon, lime & cherry

A refreshing palette cleanser, this juice makes a tasty nonalcoholic aperitif.

Thanks to its high water content, cantaloupe melon has been used for centuries in India as a diuretic. It is also loaded with digestive enzymes. The lime adds a citrus tang and increases the detoxifying action. Traditionally, cherries were used by Native Americans to help to flush out the kidneys and to soothe the stomach. The more cherries you add to this juice, the thicker it will be.

NUTRIENTS
Vitamins B3, B6, C, folate; calcium, magnesium, phosphorus, potassium; bioflavonoids; limonin

RECIPE

1 cantaloupe melon, peeled, seeded, and cut into chunks
1 lime, peeled and quartered
25 cherries, pitted

Press alternate chunks of melon and lime, and the cherries, through a juicer. Stir and drink immediately.

grapefruit & strawberry crush

NUTRIENTS
Vitamins B2, B3, B5, B6, C, K, beta-carotene, folate; copper, iodine, magnesium, manganese, potassium; bioflavonoids; pectin

A cooling and cleansing juice—perfect for summer.

The tangy taste of grapefuit complements the sweetness of the strawberries, so this crush is a real treat for the taste buds. It is also a great detoxifier. Grapefuit provides lots of pectin, soluble fiber that helps to eliminate toxins, while strawberries are high in vitamin C, potassium, and soluble fiber, which are all known for their ability to help the body to expel waste matter. This is a great juice to have at breakfast time.

RECIPE

1 grapefruit, peeled and torn into segments
1¼ cups filtered water, frozen as icecubes
10 strawberries, hulled

Press the grapefruit segments through a juicer. Crush the ice in a blender, then add the strawberries and grapefruit juice. Whiz until the strawberries are smooth and drink immediately.

lemon, apple, grape & apricot

The ultimate liver cleansers, these fab four will kick-start a sluggish system.

The vitamin C found in these fruits helps to flush alcohol out of the system, and the diuretic effect of the lemon and the fiber in the apple makes this juice a powerful detoxifier. Grapes are excellent cleansers and their high sugar content helps to restore flagging energy levels. Apricots are a natural sweetener and a laxative. Choose those with bright orange skin, as they contain more nutrients and are sweeter than pale yellow ones.

NUTRIENTS
Vitamins B1, B2, B3, B5, B6, C, K, beta-carotene, biotin, folate; calcium, iron, magnesium, manganese, phosphorus, potassium, selenium, zinc; bioflavonoids; limonin; malic acid; pectin; tryptophan

RECIPE

3 lemons, peeled and quartered
2 apples, cut into wedges
3 apricots, halved and pitted
25 red seedless grapes

Press alternate fruit chunks and the grapes through a juicer. Stir, and drink immediately.

Red grapes contain higher levels of antioxidants than white varieties.

cabbage, carrot & cranberry

NUTRIENTS
Vitamins B1, B2, B6, C, E,
K, beta-carotene, folate;
calcium, chromium, iodine,
iron, magnesium, manganese,
potassium, phosphorus

This "coleslaw in a glass" is a powerful detoxifier
that is super-rich in vitamin C.

Research shows that the phytochemicals found in cabbage are
powerful detoxifiers. The nutrients in carrots also boost the
spring-cleaning process. Thanks to the antibacterial agents
and the condensed tannins in cranberries, this juice can help to
treat and prevent urinary tract infections. Choose fresh, deep-
red berries, as they contain more of the beneficial compounds.

RECIPE

½ **medium cabbage, leaves
separated, core chopped
into chunks**
**3 large carrots, topped, tailed,
and chopped into chunks**
40 cranberries

Wrap each cabbage leaf around
a chunk of cabbage core or
carrot and press them through
a juicer, alternating with a few
cranberries. Stir and drink
immediately.

beet, grapefruit & lime

Cleanse your body with this harmonious blend of sharp citrus fruits and sweet beets.

Beets have been used as a detoxifier and blood purifier for centuries and are recommended by naturopaths as a colon cleanser. Limonoids—phytochemicals found in grapefruits—help to form a detoxifying enzyme, which the liver utilizes to make toxic compounds more water-soluble, thereby flushing them out of the body more effectively. Limes have an alkalizing effect, which also helps to eliminate waste.

NUTRIENTS

Vitamin C, beta-carotene, biotin, folate; calcium, iron, magnesium, manganese, phosphorus, potassium; bioflavonoids; limonin; lycopene; pectin

RECIPE

3 small beets, chopped into chunks
1 grapefruit, peeled and torn into segments
2 limes, peeled and quartered

Press alternate chunks of beet, grapefruit, and lime through a juicer. Stir and drink immediately.

Avoid grapefruit juice when taking medication, as it can boost the potency of some prescription drugs.

007

⊗ ⊗ ⊘ ◐ ✪ ✿

beet, carrot & apple

NUTRIENTS
Vitamins B, C, K, beta-carotene, biotin, folate; calcium, chromium, iron, magnesium, manganese, phosphorus, potassium; malic acid; pectin

Betacyanin, the pigment that gives beets their rich purple colour, can turn urine harmlessly pink or orange.

Bursting with waste-flushing nutrients, this bright red juice is the ultimate detoxifier.

Too much processed food and alcohol overload the body, leading to lethargy and bloating. Counteract these effects with this juice containing three of nature's finest detoxifying ingredients to leave you feeling lighter and brighter.

Beet An excellent intestinal, liver, and digestive-tract cleanser, beets are a powerhouse of nutrients that are especially effective when eaten raw or drunk as a juice. They are particularly rich in biotin, a water-soluble B-vitamin that plays a key part in metabolizing proteins, fats, and carbohydrates.

RECIPE

3 small beets, chopped into chunks
2 large carrots, topped, tailed, and chopped into chunks
2 apples, cut into wedges

Press alternate chunks of beet, carrot, and apple through a juicer. Stir and drink immediately.

Carrot One of the top detoxifiers of the vegetable world, carrot helps to boost the function of the liver, kidneys, and digestive system. Raw carrot juice is a gentle remedy for fluid retention, bloating, digestive sluggishness, and the general feeling of fatigue that follows a period of unhealthy living.

Apple One medium, unpeeled apple provides a good dose of our recommended daily fiber intake. For a sweet juice, use red apples, or for a tarter flavor, use green ones.

PREPARATION TIPS

• Choose beets that are firm, smooth-skinned and deeply colored and remember small-to-medium roots taste sweeter than larger ones.

• Prevent staining your skin red by wearing latex gloves when you chop beets. If you do stain your fingers or nails, rub a slice of lemon—a natural bleaching agent—over the affected area.

• Studies show that pesticides are absorbed into the skin of carrots, so always peel them before juicing, unless they are organic.

• If you store apples in the refrigerator, they will retain their crisp texture for approximately one month.

carrot, lemon & flax seed oil

NUTRIENTS
Vitamins C, K, beta-carotene, folate; calcium, chromium, iron, magnesium, potassium; alpha-linolenic acid; bioflavonoids; lignans; limonin; omega-3 and omega-6 fatty acids

Drinking this zingy juice on an empty stomach kick-starts a sluggish digestive system.

Carrots and lemons make a great partnership for detoxifying, as their cleansing nutrients work well together and the sugars in the carrots soften the sharpness of the lemons. This tasty combination also helps to make the flax seed oil more palatable. Adding this oil increases the juice's cleansing action, thanks to its gentle effect on the digestive process. Flax seed oil is also rich in alpha-linolenic acid, an important source of essential fatty acids.

RECIPE

4 large carrots, topped, tailed, and chopped into chunks
2 lemons, peeled and quartered
1 tbsp. flax seed oil

Press alternate chunks of carrot and lemon through a juicer. Stir in the oil and drink immediately.

cucumber, celery & broccoli

This bright-green super-juice is an excellent cleansing cocktail and is seriously good for you.

These three green vegetables combine to make an extremely powerful detoxifier. The ascorbic and caffeic acids in cucumber prevent water retention, yet at the same time its high water content rehydrates the system. Raw celery juice works wonders at reducing puffiness and canceling out the fermentation process of any alcohol in the system, while broccoli cleanses the intestines and stimulates the liver.

NUTRIENTS

Vitamins B1, B2, B3, B5, B6, C, E, beta-carotene, folate; calcium, iron, magnesium, manganese, phosphorus, potassium, silica, zinc; tryptophan

RECIPE

1 cucumber, chopped
  into chunks
3 celery stalks including tops,
  chopped into chunks
2 medium broccoli flowerets,
  chopped into chunks

Press alternate chunks of vegetables through a juicer, stir, and drink immediately.

The ancient Greeks used the leaves of the celery plant as laurels to decorate their renowned athletes.

tomato, onion & lemon

NUTRIENTS
Vitamins B1, B2, B3, B5, B6,
C, E, K, beta-carotene, folate;
calcium, chromium, copper,
iron, magnesium, manganese,
phosphorus, potassium; sulfur;
bioflavonoids; limonin; tryptophan

Full of goodness, this trio of ingredients alkalizes, rebalances, and detoxifies the body.

Made up of more than 90 percent water, raw tomatoes neutralize acid and help to reduce liver inflammation. Onions are rich in powerful sulfur compounds, which are responsible for their pungent odor and many of their health-promoting effects, such as helping to flush heavy metals and toxins out of the system. Adding the lemon turbo-charges the cleansing properties of the juice and makes the onion taste more palatable.

RECIPE

**4 large tomatoes, cut
into wedges
1 onion, peeled and cut
into wedges
2 lemons, peeled and
quartered**

Press alternate chunks of
tomato, onion and lemon
through a juicer. Stir and
drink immediately.

watercress, cucumber, broccoli & tarragon

This peppery juice is a great digestive cleanser.

Watercress is one of the best foods for purifying the blood, and relieving phlegm. Cucumber is cleansing and broccoli provides nutrients that assist the body's own healing and detoxifying processes. The liquoricelike flavor of tarragon peps up the juice. The herb also contains iodine, which aids digestion and helps to speed up the elimination of toxins.

NUTRIENTS
Vitamins B1, B2, B3, B5, B6, C, E, K, beta-carotene, folate; calcium, iodine, iron, magnesium, manganese, phosphorus, potassium, zinc; tryptophan

RECIPE

2 medium broccoli flowerets, chopped into chunks
½ cucumber, chopped into chunks
1 large bunch watercress
8 fresh tarragon leaves

Press alternate chunks of broccoli and cucumber through a juicer. Combine the watercress, tarragon, and juice in a blender and whiz until smooth. Drink immediately.

If you find the taste of this juice too strong, try diluting it with an equal amount of water.

apple, apricot & cinnamon

NUTRIENTS

Vitamins B2, B3, B5, C, K, beta-carotene; calcium, iron, magnesium, manganese, phosphorus, potassium, zinc; malic acid; pectin; tryptophan

Naturally sweet, this nutritious juice is a healthy way to satisfy a sweet tooth.

Apples derive most of their natural sweetness from fructose, a simple sugar the body breaks down slowly. Combined with a hefty dose of soluble fiber, this helps to keep blood sugar levels stable and to prevent cravings. Apricots are deliciously filling, while cinnamon contains volatile oils, which improve the body's ability to utilize blood sugar. This helps to prevent blood glucose dips, which are linked to low energy levels and the desire for a high-calorie, diet-breaking treat.

RECIPE

4 apples, cut into wedges
3 apricots, halved and pitted
½ tsp. ground cinnamon

Press alternate chunks of apple and apricot through a juicer and stir. Sprinkle the cinnamon over and drink immediately.

apple, grape & pomegranate

Fruits full of fiber and with a high water content are excellent for aiding weight loss.

Research shows that pectin, the soluble fiber in apples, has more power to knock the edge off appetite than ordinary fiber. The high water content of the grapes can aid weight loss because rehydrating the body boosts the metabolic rate—the faster the metabolism works, the quicker we burn up calories, making weight gain less likely. Pomegranate seeds are also packed with hunger-curbing fiber.

NUTRIENTS

Vitamins B1, B3, B6, C, E, K, beta-carotene, biotin, folate; calcium, magnesium, manganese, phosphorus, potassium, selenium, zinc; malic acid; pectin

RECIPE

4 apples, cut into wedges
25 seedless grapes
1 pomegranate, cut in half

Press alternate chunks of apple, and the grapes through a juicer. Tap the pomegranate on the skin side with a wooden spoon to remove the seeds, and add to the juice. Stir and drink immediately.

In Greek mythology, the pomegranate represents life, regeneration, and marriage.

plum, pear & fig

NUTRIENTS
Vitamins B2, C, beta-carotene, folate; calcium, copper, iodine, iron, magnesium, manganese, phosphorus, potassium; tryptophan

Stave off hunger pangs with this tasty combination, which is especially high in soluble fiber.

Plums are packed with natural sugars and soluble fiber, which produce a feeling of fullness that can help to prevent overeating. In one study, women who significantly increased their soluble fiber intake ate less, yet their hunger did not increase. Easily digested, pears contain pectin and help the body to eliminate cholesterol. Figs are one of the richest plant sources of calcium and are often recommended as part of a weight-management program.

Along with peaches and nectarines, plums are drupes — fruits with a hard pit surrounding their seeds.

RECIPE

4 plums, halved
   and pitted
3 large ripe pears,
   chopped into chunks
2 figs, stems removed

Press alternate pieces of fruit through a juicer. Stir and drink immediately.

watermelon, peach & pomegranate

Sweet and thick, this low-calorie juice is particularly refreshing served over ice in a tall glass.

NUTRIENTS
Vitamins B1, B3, B6, C, E, beta-carotene, folate, calcium, magnesium, phosphorus, potassium; bioflavonoids

Watermelon is a superb diuretic. Juicing the seeds, as well as the flesh, boosts its fiber content and weight-stabilizing qualities. Peaches are also diuretic and cleanse the digestive tract, encouraging weight loss. For a smoother texture, juice the pomegranate with the other fruit. The seeds will be ejected with the pulp.

RECIPE

½ watermelon, peeled and
  chopped into chunks
2 peaches, pitted
  and quartered
1 pomegranate, cut in half

Press alternate chunks of watermelon and peach through a juicer. Tap the pomegranate on the skin side with a wooden spoon to remove the seeds and add to the juice. Drink immediately.

grapefruit, melon & raspberry

NUTRIENTS
Vitamins B2, B3, B6, C,
beta-carotene, folate; calcium,
copper, magnesium, manganese,
phosphorus, potassium, zinc;
bioflavonoids; pectin

This is a nutritious, thirst-quenching combination that won't notch up many calories.

Keeping your fluid intake consistently high is a key principle of successful weight loss, because it prevents the body from confusing thirst with hunger and helps the digestive system to work efficiently. The fructose in the melon supplies an instant source of energy. The sweet raspberry juice balances the sourness of the grapefruit and provides soluble fiber, as well as calcium, which is a useful mineral for weight loss as it helps to boost the body's fat-burning ability.

Raspberries are loaded with ellagic acid, an antioxidant with powerful anti-carcinogenic properties.

RECIPE

1 grapefruit, peeled and torn
   into segments
1 melon, peeled, seeded, and
   chopped into chunks
15 raspberries

Press alternate chunks
of fruit, and the raspberries
through a juicer. Stir and
drink immediately.

blackberry & yogurt smoothie

Delicious, filling, and packed with nutrients, this drink makes an ideal breakfast for slimmers.

Blackberries are an excellent source of fiber, as they contain the soluble fiber pectin, as well as many small seeds—each blackberry is made up of a cluster of tiny fruits housing a seed. Research links consumption of low-fat, calcium-rich dairy products, such as yogurt, to lower body-fat ratios. And studies show eating almonds increases weight loss, because their high monounsaturated fat content helps the body to burn fat.

NUTRIENTS
Vitamins A, B2, B3, B5, B12, C, D, E, beta-carotene, folate; calcium, copper, iron, magnesium, manganese, phosphorus, potassium, selenium, zinc; tryptophan

RECIPE

25 blackberries
1¾ cups plain yogurt with
 live bacteria
a generous sprinkling of
 almond flakes

Whiz the berries and yogurt together in a blender until smooth. Sprinkle the almond flakes over and drink immediately.

⊛⊗❂★✷

grapefruit, honey, lemon & ginger

NUTRIENTS

Vitamins B6, C, D, E, K, beta-carotene, folate; calcium, copper, iodine, iron, magnesium, manganese, phosphorus, potassium, sodium, sulfur, zinc; bioflavonoids; limonin; pectin

---

RECIPE

2 grapefruit, peeled and broken into segments
3 lemons, peeled and quartered
1 large knob (1½ in.) fresh gingerroot, peeled and cut into chunks
1 tbsp. honey

Press alternate chunks of grapefruit, lemon, and ginger through a juicer. Add the honey, stir well, and drink immediately.

This tongue-tingling juice is a great fat burner and also helps to regulate blood-sugar levels.

These ingredients provide a powerful combination of digestive enzymes to aid weight loss. Drink the juice before breakfast on an empty stomach for maximum fat-burning effect. The four strong flavors, which complement each other perfectly, also have a wonderful warming effect that helps to soothe a sore throat and help your body to fight off a cold or an infection.

Grapefruit Research confirms that grapefruit contains a fat-burning enzyme and helps to prevent weight gain by lowering insulin levels and keeping blood-sugar levels stable. It also provides a substantial amount of the soluble fiber, pectin.

Honey Adding honey softens the sharp citrus taste of the lemon and grapefruit, and increases the nutritional value of the juice. Manuka honey has been found to contain the highest number of active enzymes with healing properties.

Lemon The juice from lemons boosts overall liver function, helping the digestive system to become more efficient at processing food, so the body stores less fat.

Gingerroot This spice helps to tone the muscles of the digestive tract, triggers enzyme activity, and increases the secretion of digestive juices in the stomach, which means dietary fats are more likely to be used rather than stored. Ginger also boosts the circulation and metabolism, and contains manganese, which supports the immune system and fights infections.

PREPARATION TIPS

• Rolling a grapefruit or a lemon under the palm of your hand on the counter before juicing it will help you to extract more juice.

• A soft spot at the stem end of a grapefruit is a sign it is past its best, but scratches or scales on the skin do not affect its taste or quality.

• Store honey in an airtight container so it doesn't absorb moisture from the air, and it will keep almost indefinitely.

• Keep any unused gingerroot fresh by storing it in the freezer wrapped in plastic wrap.

The origin of the name "grapefruit" comes from the way the fruit grows — hanging in clusters like grapes.

leek, carrot & cabbage

NUTRIENTS
Vitamins B1, B2, B6, C, E, K, beta-carotene, folate; calcium, chromium, iodine, iron, magnesium, manganese, potassium, phosphorus

Drink a glass of this powerful juice every day to help blast the fat stores around your abdomen.

The combination of nutrients in leeks means they slow the absorption of sugars from the intestinal tract, which stabilizes blood-sugar levels and dampens hunger pangs. The process of transforming the beta-carotene in carrots into vitamin A in the intestines speeds up metabolism and removes fat deposits quicker. Cabbage contains both sulfur and iodine, which cleanse the intestines and break up stored fat.

Choose small leeks, as they are more nutritious than the larger, more fiberous varieties.

RECIPE

½ medium cabbage, leaves separated and core chopped into chunks
1 leek, topped, tailed, and chopped into chunks
4 large carrots, topped, tailed, and chopped into chunks

Wrap each cabbage leaf around a chunk of leek or carrot and press through a juicer. Stir and drink immediately.

onion, spinach & red pepper

This juice combines three seriously fat-busting ingredients in one great-tasting mix.

Low in calories, onions boast several minerals and oils that help to break down fat deposits and speed up metabolism. They also contain quercetin, a cancer-fighting antioxidant. Spinach is an excellent source of many nutrients linked to weight loss, including calcium and iron. Bell peppers, even mild-tasting ones, contain substances that significantly increase heat production in the body for more than 20 minutes after they are eaten, which burns up calories quicker. Grating a little aromatic nutmeg over the juice can help to lift the strong flavor of the onion and sometimes bitter taste of the raw spinach.

NUTRIENTS
Vitamins B1, B2, B3, B6, C, E, K, folate; calcium, chromium, copper, iodine, iron, magnesium, manganese, phosphorus, potassium, zinc; bioflavonoids; quercetin; sulfur compounds; tryptophan

RECIPE

10½ oz. spinach leaves
2 onions, peeled and cut
  into wedges
1 red bell pepper, seeded
  and chopped into chunks
a little freshly grated nutmeg

Wrap the spinach leaves around chunks of onion and pepper. Press alternate vegetables through a juicer, and stir. Sprinkle the grated nutmeg over and drink immediately.

cucumber, celery, pumpkin & fennel

NUTRIENTS
Vitamins B1, B2, B3, B5, B6, C, beta-carotene, folate; calcium, chromium, cobalt, iron, magnesium, manganese, phosphorus, potassium, selenium, silicon, sodium, sulfur, zinc; tryptophan

Avoid cucumber if you are allergic to pollen or aspirin, as it can make your mouth itchy.

Exceptionally low in calories and rich in nutrients, this juice gets you back on track after a binge.

One serving of this juice is refreshing and filling, yet contains only 100 calories and no fat. Not only will it help to reduce hunger in between meals, but it also aids the body with digesting high-fat, high-protein foods. Serve the juice with a stalk of celery in the glass that can act as an edible stirrer.

Cucumber The sulfur and silicon in cucumber stimulate the kidneys to wash out uric acid—triggering the flushing out of stored fat, assisted by the high water content.

RECIPE

½ cucumber, chopped into chunks
3 celery stalks including tops, chopped into chunks
½ pumpkin, peeled, seeded, and chopped into chunks
2 fennel bulbs, quartered

Press alternate chunks of cucumber, celery, pumpkin, and fennel through a juicer. Stir and drink immediately.

Celery Raw celery juice clocks up very few, low-density calories and stimulates the pituitary gland, which regulates the body's energy consumption. It is also rich in selenium, a trace mineral needed to activate the thyroid to boost metabolism.

Pumpkin One study found that including pumpkin in the diet helps to curb the appetite. The participants of the study also absorbed less fat and calories from their food.

Fennel Recommended for weight loss by many nutritionists, fennel has appetite-suppressing properties and an ability to create a sensation of "fullness" in the stomach.

PREPARATION TIPS

• Look for firm cucumbers with a rich green color and without any soft spots. Avoid ones that bulge in the middle—they are likely to be tasteless.

• Choose celery that looks crisp and snaps easily when pulled apart.

• Good quality fennel has whitish or pale-green bulbs that are firm and solid, without any splits, bruises, or spots. Fresh fennel smells faintly of licorice.

• The different parts of fennel—the base, stems, and leaves—can all be used in the recipe opposite.

asparagus, celery & carrot

NUTRIENTS
Vitamins B1, B2, B3, B6, C, K, beta-carotene, folate; calcium, copper, chromium, iron, magnesium, manganese, phosphorus, potassium, selenium; asparagine; tryptophan

This refreshing juice helps your body to banish fat and is an ideal drink after a workout.

Asparagus has less than four calories per spear and contains the amino acid asparagine, which is excellent at breaking down fat. It also works as a powerful diuretic, helping to reduce weight-adding water retention. Celery has a high water content, an average of only three calories per stalk and is a great source of rehydration after exercise. The beta-carotene in carrots triggers the fat-flushing process and helps to stabilize blood-sugar levels.

RECIPE

10 asparagus spears, chopped into chunks
6 celery stalks including tops, chopped into chunks
2 large carrots, topped, tailed, and chopped into chunks

Press alternate chunks of vegetable through a juicer, stir, and drink immediately.

tomato, celery, garlic & basil

The taste of Italy in a glass—and with far fewer calories than pizza!

Tomatoes contain enzymes that prompt the kidneys to filter out large quantities of fatty deposits and eliminate them. Raw celery has a high concentration of easily digestible calcium, which also helps to remove fat. Allicin, the potent active constituent in garlic, has been shown to prevent weight gain. Basil leaves add sweetness, as well as iron, which boosts energy levels and will stop you reaching for fatty snacks.

NUTRIENTS
Vitamins B1, B2, B3, B5, B6, C, E, K, beta-carotene, folate, calcium, chromium, copper, iron, magnesium, manganese, phosphorus, potassium, selenium; lycopene; tryptophan

RECIPE

4 large tomatoes, cut
   into wedges
3 celery stalks including tops,
   chopped into chunks
2 cloves garlic, peeled
a handful fresh basil

Wrap the basil leaves around pieces of tomato, celery and garlic, press through a juicer. Stir and drink immediately.

Never juice the leaves of the tomato plant, as they contain toxic alkaloids.

watercress, arugula & tomato

NUTRIENTS
Vitamins B1, B2, B3, B5, B6,
C, E, K, beta-carotene, folate;
calcium, chromium, copper, iodine,
iron, magnesium, manganese,
phosphorus, potassium; lycopene;
sulphoranphane; tryptophan

An excellent diet aid, this trio is exceptionally high in nutrients, yet very low in calories.

Traditionally, watercress has been used to boost metabolism and detoxify the body. It is the richest natural source of glucosinolate—a phytochemical that boosts the liver's detoxification enzymes, helping to flush out the system and, in turn, promote weight loss. Arugula leaves were used by the ancient Greeks to soothe digestion; and they are also a good source of glucosinolates. Tomatoes are one of nature's super-cleansers. For maximum flavor, remove them from the refrigerator 30 minutes before you use them.

RECIPE

1 large bunch watercress
3 oz. arugula leaves
5 large tomatoes, cut
  into wedges

Wrap leaves around chunks of
tomato, press through a juicer,
stir, and drink immediately.

watercress & yogurt smoothie

This pale-green, savory smoothie makes a good replacement for a meal on a busy day.

The high iron content of the watercress is useful for dieters, as low levels of iron can lead to fatigue and cravings for unhealthy foods. Low-fat yogurt is a great source of calcium and has a low glycemic index (GI), which means it provides the body with slow-burning fuel to help to reduce hunger between meals. Cayenne pepper stimulates the flow of stomach secretions, which aids digestion. It also speeds up metabolism immediately after consumption.

NUTRIENTS

Vitamins A, B1, B2, B3, B5, B12, C, D, E, K, beta-carotene, folate; calcium, copper, iodine, iron, magnesium, manganese, phosphorus, potassium, zinc

RECIPE

1 large bunch watercress
1¾ cups plain yogurt with
**   live bacteria**
a pinch cayenne pepper

Whiz the watercress and yogurt together in a blender until you have a smooth consistency. Sprinkle a little cayenne pepper over and drink immediately.

Use low-fat milk instead of yogurt to make a smoothie with a thinner consistency.

blackberry, apple & pineapple

NUTRIENTS

Vitamins B1, B2, B6, C, E, K, beta-carotene, folate; calcium, copper, iron, magnesium, manganese, phosphorus, potassium, selenium, zinc; bromelain; malic acid; pectin

A fruity combination that gives you get-up-and-go.

Blackberries have the highest level of phytoestrogens in the berry world and are bursting with vitamin C, which helps to perk up energy levels when your body needs an extra boost. Freshly squeezed apple juice also contains vitamin C, as well as fructose, and malic acid, all of which aid energy production. Known for its anti-inflammatory properties, pineapple is an excellent source of manganese, which is used by energy-making enzymes. One cup of fresh pineapple supplies exceptionally high levels of this mineral.

Traditionally, blackberries have been used to treat sore throats and laryngitis.

RECIPE

25 blackberries
2 apples, cut into wedges
1 pineapple, peeled and chopped into chunks

Press alternate blackberries and chunks of fruit through a juicer. Stir and drink immediately.

peach, apricot & mango

This soft fruit salad in liquid form provides a delicious, super-fast energy fix.

Naturally rich in fructose for instant energy, peaches and apricots make a thick-textured juice rich in many nutrients, including phosphorus and vitamin B5, which both help the body to utilize energy from food. Mango is high in beta-carotene and provides some iron, too. If you are feeling very tired, use dried apricots instead of fresh ones, as they contain more fructose, beta-carotene, potassium and iron, making them a fantastic source of energy.

NUTRIENTS
Vitamins B2, B3, B5, C, E, beta-carotene, folate; calcium, iron, magnesium, phosphorus, potassium, zinc; bioflavonoids; tryptophan

RECIPE

**3 peaches, quartered
and pitted
3 apricots, halved
and pitted
1 mango, peeled, pitted and
chopped into chunks**

Press alternate chunks of fruit through a juicer, stir, and drink immediately.

watermelon, fig & honey

NUTRIENTS
Vitamins B1, B2, B3, B5, B6, C,
D, E, K, beta-carotene, folate;
calcium, iodine, iron, magnesium,
manganese, phosphorus,
potassium, sulfur; tryptophan

If you suffer from a midafternoon energy slump, revive yourself instantly with this sweet treat.

Watermelons have a high level of natural sugars, making them an ideal source of instant energy, and their high water content is rehydrating, helping to prevent fatigue. Traditionally, figs are used as a sweetener, because they have a high glucose and fructose content—two simple sugars that are easily assimilated and help to boost energy. For a super-energizing option, use dried figs, as they contain more sugar. Honey also contains glucose and fructose.

RECIPE

½ **watermelon, peeled, seeded, and chopped into chunks**
3 medium figs, stems removed
1 tbsp. honey

Press alternate chunks of watermelon and fig through a juicer, add the honey, stir well, and drink immediately.

blueberry, pomegranate & soymilk smoothie

A delicious smoothie to top up your tank anytime.

Blueberries are loaded with phytochemicals and help to lower cholesterol and protect against disease. Made up of 43 percent protein, soymilk is cholesterol-free and rich in isoflavones—antioxidants said to protect the body against free radicals. Pomegranate juice contains more energy-preserving antioxidants than red wine or green tea. And one pomegranate supplies 40 percent of an adult's daily vitamin C requirement.

NUTRIENTS
Vitamins A, B2, B3, B12, C, D, E, K, beta-carotene, folate; calcium, iodine, iron, magnesium, manganese, phosphorus, potassium; isoflavones; tryptophan

RECIPE

40 blueberries
2 cups soymilk
1 pomegranate, cut in half

Whiz together the berries and milk in a blender until smooth. Tap the pomegranate on the skin side with a wooden spoon to remove the seeds. Add to the mix, stir, and drink immediately.

Use frozen berries straight from the freezer to create a deliciously cold smoothie.

banana & chocolate shake

NUTRIENTS
Vitamins B2, B12, D, K, calcium, chromium, copper, folate, iodine, iron, magnesium, manganese, phosphorus, potassium, zinc; flavonoids; omega-3 fatty acids; tryptophan

This tastes delicious and is a great pick-me-up.

Instantly available calories from the chocolate and the slower-releasing calories from bananas make this milkshake an ideal battery recharger, especially before physical activity.

Banana This fruit is one of the few to contain chromium, a mineral essential for the metabolism of cholesterol, fats, and proteins, and energy production. Bananas also have a high level of carbohydrate, which is filling and a good source of fuel.

Chocolate The dark variety containing at least 70 percent cocoa has lower levels of fat and sugar than milk or white chocolate

> The Aztec emperor, Montezuma, described chocolate as, "the divine drink that builds up resistance and fights fatigue."

RECIPE

2 cups milk
1 oz. dark chocolate, broken
   into pieces
2 ripe bananas, peeled

Gently heat the milk in a saucepan, never allowing it to boil. Stir in the chocolate until it melts. Whiz together the banana and chocolate milk in a blender until smooth and drink immediately.

and is loaded with nutritional benefits. Rich in flavonoids, which fight free radicals, dark chocolate boosts blood antioxidant levels by 20 percent. It also contains energy-boosting caffeine and phenylethylamine, which is a mild mood elevator.

Milk Cow's milk is a good source of vitamin D, calcium, and vitamin K—three nutrients essential for bone health. It contains low-fat protein, as well as vitamins B2 and B12, which are crucial for energy production.

PREPARATION TIPS

- Unripe bananas should not be placed in the refrigerator, as this will interrupt the ripening process and they will remain green even if returned to room temperature.

- Riper bananas make a smoother drink and are more easily digested by the body, so opt for those that are soft and have yellow skins mottled with brown.

- Recent research shows that organic cow's milk contains 70 percent more omega-3 fatty acids than nonorganic milk.

- Avoid storing milk in the refrigerator door, as this exposes it to heat each time the door is opened, and can cause it to become sour.

031

apple, carrot & spirulina

NUTRIENTS
Vitamins B2, B3, B6, B12, C, E, K, beta-carotene, folate; calcium, chromium, iron, magnesium, phosphorus, potassium, sodium; chlorophyll; gamma-linoleic acid; malic acid; pectin

For instant energy, try this variation on the apple and carrot classic with a super-nutritious twist.

The highly concentrated sugars in fresh apple and carrot juice are easily absorbed for on-the-spot energy. Spirulina is a blue-green vegetable algae full of energy-boosting nutrients. Freeze-dried powder retains the most nutrients: 58 times more iron than raw spinach; 25 times more beta-carotene than raw carrots; three times more vitamin E than raw wheat germ, plus the essential fatty acid gamma-linolenic acid (GLA), chlorophyll, and vitamin B12.

RECIPE

4 apples, cut into wedges
3 large carrots, topped, tailed, and chopped into chunks
2 tsp. powdered spirulina

Press alternate chunks of carrot and apple through a juicer. Stir one teaspoonful of spirulina into each glass of juice and drink immediately.

avocado, plum & pear

Deliciously sweet and thick, this juice is the ideal fuel-providing stomach-liner before a night out.

Avocados contain more protein than any other fruit, making them a great source of energy. Just one provides around half the recommended daily intake of vitamin B6—essential for helping the body to release energy from food. Soft ripe plums and pears are bursting with fructose, which the body easily absorbs and converts into energy. Plums are also a good source of iron, as well as malic acid, which enhances the absorption of iron.

NUTRIENTS
Vitamins B1, B2, B3, B5, B6, C, E, K, beta-carotene, biotin, folate; calcium, copper, iodine, iron, magnesium, phosphorus, potassium, zinc; malic acid; omega-6 fatty acids; tryptophan

RECIPE

6 plums, pitted and halved
2 large ripe pears, chopped into chunks
1 avocado, peeled and pitted

Press alternate chunks of plum and pear through a juicer. Whiz together the plum and pear juice with the avocado in a blender until smooth and drink immediately.

Choose an avocado at the peak of its ripeness for an extra smooth, textured juice.

cucumber, lime & spirulina

NUTRIENTS
Vitamins B2, B6, B12, C, E,
beta-carotene, folate;
calcium, iron, magnesium,
manganese, potassium, silica;
bioflavonoids; gamma-linolenic
acid; limonin; tryptophan

A palate-tingling treat which helps to prevent dehydration—a common cause of fatigue.

Humans are made up of around 75 percent water and even a two percent loss can result in a 20 percent drop in energy levels. Thanks to the high water content of the cucumber and lime juice, this recipe tops up hydration and gives a quick energy boost. Research shows spirulina has a positive effect on the immune system, too, boosting resistance to disease.

Take spirulina in the morning, as some people find it can keep them awake if taken later in the day.

RECIPE

1 cucumber, chopped
  into chunks
3 limes, peeled and
  quartered
2 tsp. powdered spirulina

Press alternate chunks of cucumber and lime through a juicer. Stir one teaspoonful of spirulina into each glass of juice, stir again, and drink immediately.

squash, Brussels sprout & wheat grass

Adding a shot or spoonful of wheat grass catapults the health-boosting benefits of this juice into orbit.

Squash is rich in carotenoids to help regulate blood sugar and keep energy levels constant. Brussels sprouts, with their high vitamin C and folate content, also help to replenish energy stores. Obtain wheat grass from a health food store or juice it yourself using a masticating juicer (see page 8). Wheat grass contains more than 100 key nutrients, such as amino acids, enzymes, minerals, vitamins, and chlorophyll.

NUTRIENTS
Vitamins B1, B2, B3, B5, B6, C, E, K, beta-carotene, folate; boron, calcium, chloride, chromium, cobalt, copper, iodine, iron, magnesium, manganese, phosphorus, potassium, selenium, sodium, sulfur, zinc; amino acids; chlorophyll; tryptophan

RECIPE

1 squash, peeled, seeded and chopped into chunks
10 Brussels sprouts
2 tbsp. wheat grass powder or store-bought juice

Press alternate chunks of squash, and Brussels sprouts through a juicer and add a tablespoonful of wheat grass powder or juice to each glass. Stir and drink immediately.

⊛⊗⊛★✩🗩

orange, kiwi fruit & spinach

NUTRIENTS
Vitamins B1, B2, B3, B5, B6,
C, E, K, beta-carotene, folate;
calcium, copper, iodine, iron,
magnesium, manganese,
phosphorus, potassium, zinc;
bioflavonoids; limonin

Juicing, rather
than squeezing,
oranges means
you benefit from
the bioflavonoids
in the pith.

One glass of this energizing OJ drink provides nearly three times our daily vitamin C requirement.

A lack of iron can lead to lethargy and depression, and it is one of the most common mineral deficiencies in the world. This juice notches up iron absorption. It also boosts the level of folate in the body, which is necessary for the production of red blood cells to restore energy to optimum levels.

Orange This fruit is packed with vitamin C, a very powerful antioxidant that greatly improves the body's ability to absorb dietary iron, thus helping to relieve iron-deficient anemia. Oranges also contain limonin, which not only has

---

RECIPE

10½ oz. spinach leaves
2 oranges, peeled and torn
    into segments
3 kiwi fruit, peeled and
    chopped into chunks

Wrap the spinach leaves around chunks of orange and kiwi fruit. Press through a juicer, stir, and drink immediately.

anticarcinogenic properties, but is also attached to a glucose molecule, which the body easily digests and uses as energy.

Kiwi Fruit Boasting almost twice as much vitamin C as an orange, kiwi fruit is also a good source of magnesium and vitamin E, and contains copper, which is needed to make energy.

Spinach A useful source of iron, spinach is also packed with energy-restoring folate and vitamins B1, B6, C, and E. Vitamin B1 is involved in the conversion of carbohydrates into energy.

PREPARATION TIPS

• Thin-skinned oranges contain more juice than those that are thick-skinned.

• Place oranges in a bowl of warm water for several minutes before juicing and they will provide more juice.

• Select kiwi fruits that yield slightly to pressure when held between your thumb and forefinger. Those that are very soft, shriveled or have damp spots are overripe.

• Choose vibrant, deep-green spinach leaves without any signs of yellowing, wilting, or bruising, and wash them carefully immediately before use to remove any dirt and grit.

beet, green bean & pumpkin

NUTRIENTS
Vitamins B1, B2, B3, C, K,
beta-carotene, biotin, folate;
calcium, copper, iron, magnesium,
manganese, phosphorus,
potassium; malic acid; tryptophan

This invigorating combination combats tiredness.

Beets, including the tops, are full of iron and have traditionally been used as a remedy for fatigue and anemia. An important component of the blood, iron is crucial for energy production. Green beans contain almost twice as much iron as spinach, as well as the vitamins B1 and B2 needed to process carbohydrates, fats, and proteins. Pumpkin contains malic acid, which boosts iron absorption.

RECIPE

**3 small beets, chopped
into chunks**
**25 green beans, topped
and tailed**
**½ pumpkin, peeled, seeded,
and cut into chunks**

Press alternate chunks of
vegetable through a juicer,
stir, and drink immediately.

pepper, carrot, lettuce & alfalfa sprout

Revive your get-up-and-go with this energizing juice, overflowing with health-boosting enzymes.

The natural sugars in the bell pepper and carrots provide energy and soften the bitter taste of the alfalfa, which is high in protein, chlorophyll, phytochemicals, flavonoids, and phytoestrogens as well as vitamins and minerals. Juice only mature alfalfa sprouts with two sets of leaves, as nonsprouted ones contain canavanine, which is thought to trigger auto-immune disease, such as rheumatoid arthritis.

NUTRIENTS
Vitamins B1, B2, B3, B5, B6, B12, C, D, E, K, beta-carotene, folate; boron, calcium, chromium, cobalt, copper, iron, magnesium, manganese, phosphorus, potassium, silicon, sodium, sulfur, zinc; bioflavonoids; chlorophyll; phytochemicals; phytoestrogens; tryptophan

RECIPE

a handful alfalfa sprouts
½ lettuce, leaves separated
1 red bell pepper, seeded and chopped into chunks
4 large carrots, topped, tailed, and chopped into chunks

Wrap bunches of about 10 alfalfa sprouts in lettuce leaves and, alternating with chunks of pepper and carrot, press through a juicer. Stir and drink immediately.

The seeds and leaves of the alfalfa plant can be boiled to make a nutritious tea.

apple, cherry & blueberry

NUTRIENTS
Vitamins C, E, K, beta-carotene;
calcium, iron, magnesium,
manganese, phosphorus,
potassium; anthocyanins;
bioflavonoids; pectin

This delicious, health-giving juice can help to prevent many stress-related conditions.

Apples and cherries contain high levels of health-boosting flavonoids, that have been linked with better lung function and a lower incidence of asthma, which can be triggered by stress. Anthocyanins, the antioxidants in cherries, have been found to block inflammatory enzymes and help to reduce pain. One study found evidence that consuming blueberries can help to relax the arteries and reduce the risks of cardiovascular disease, often associated with stress.

Blueberries contain at least five types of anthocyanins, the antioxidants which give them their color.

RECIPE

4 apples, cut into wedges
25 cherries, pitted
40 blueberries

Press chunks of apple, and the cherries and blueberries through a juicer. Stir and drink immediately.

039

raspberry, plum & ginger

Stress and PMS often go hand-in-hand. This tasty tonic helps to relieve premenstrual symptoms.

Raspberries are a powerhouse of nutrients and can help to ease menstrual cramps and balance mood swings. Combining them with plums gives this juice high levels of infection-fighting vitamin C, plus beta-carotene and manganese—important immunity-boosters during stressful times. As well as relieving menstrual cramps and nausea, gingerroot offers protection from heart disease, which is often stress-related, by helping to boost circulation and prevent blood clotting.

NUTRIENTS
Vitamins B2, B3, B6, C, beta-carotene, folate; calcium, copper, iron, magnesium, manganese, phosphorus, potassium, sodium, zinc

RECIPE

5 plums, halved and pitted
1 large knob (1½ in.) fresh
gingerroot, peeled and
chopped into chunks
25 raspberries

Press alternate chunks of plum and ginger, with the raspberries through a juicer. Stir and drink immediately.

apple, fig, mango & papaya

NUTRIENTS
Vitamins B3, C, E, K, beta-carotene, folate; calcium, iron, magnesium, manganese, phosphorus, potassium, silicon, sodium; malic acid; pectin

A glass of stress-relieving goodness, this super-nutritious drink calms the body and the mind.

High-fiber soft fruit provide a wide range of antistress nutrients. Apples contain vitamin C as well as magnesium, which supports the body's stress reaction. The rich supply of calcium in figs calms the mind and eases the transmission of nerve signals. Mango and papaya top up the digestive enzymes—useful when stress halts their secretion to divert energy to the brain and the muscles.

Mangoes have been shown to be the best fruit source of beta-carotene.

RECIPE

3 apples, cut into wedges
1 mango, peeled, pitted and chopped into chunks
1 papaya, peeled, seeded and chopped into chunks
2 figs, stems removed

Press alternate chunks of fruit, and the figs through a juicer. Stir and drink immediately.

strawberry, banana & peppermint crush

When it all gets too much, this soothing smoothie will banish stress and help you to relax.

The body's requirement for vitamin C increases significantly when adrenaline levels are high, yet it is the only vitamin the body cannot store. Weight for weight, strawberries contain more vitamin C than citrus fruits. The banana provides stress-relieving B-vitamins and the peppermint leaves contain menthol, a cooling and calming oil that can help to clear your head, and aid digestion.

NUTRIENTS

Vitamins B1, B2, B3, B5, B6, C, K, beta-carotene, folate; calcium, chromium, copper, iodine, iron, magnesium, manganese, potassium, selenium, sodium, zinc; bioflavonoids; tryptophan

RECIPE

1¼ cups filtered water, frozen as icecubes
15 strawberries, hulled
2 ripe bananas, peeled
1 handful fresh peppermint leaves

Crush the ice in a blender, add the strawberries, bananas and mint. Whiz until smooth and drink immediately.

tofu & raspberry smoothie

NUTRIENTS
Vitamins A, B2, B3, C, E, K, folate; calcium, copper, iron, magnesium, manganese, phosphorus, potassium, selenium, zinc; malic acid; phytochemicals; tryptophan

A tofu and fruit smoothie is a delicious and calm-inducing start to any day.

Made from the curds of soybean, tofu is an excellent source of protein and is virtually free from saturated fat. Rich in selenium, iron, and calcium to ease the nervous system, tofu also acts to balance hormones and, in doing so, can make you feel more harmonious and less stressed. Raspberries bump up the intake of antioxidants and phytochemicals and, along with vanilla, add flavor.

RECIPE

14 oz silken tofu
25 raspberries
1 vanilla bean
a generous sprinkling of
   almond slivers

Whiz together the tofu and raspberries in a blender until smooth. Score the vanilla pod lengthwise, scrape the tiny black seeds into the juice, and stir well. Sprinkle the almond slivers over, and drink immediately.

Tofu originated in China about two thousand years ago.

banana, date, apricot & yogurt smoothie

This juice is great for soothing a troubled mind.

Packed with essential, stress-busting B-vitamins and folate, this delicious juice aids the production of neurotransmitters, the brain's chemical messengers that boost clear thinking and a feeling of calm. Bananas are a rich source of potassium, which the body digests quickly and loses when we are under pressure. Dates and apricots provide an instant burst of energy, making you feel more alert and able to deal with difficult situations.

NUTRIENTS
Vitamins A, B1, B2, B3, B5, B6, B12, C, D, K, beta-carotene, folate; calcium, chromium, iodine, iron, magnesium, manganese, phosphorus, potassium, selenium, zinc; tryptophan

RECIPE

2 bananas, peeled
2 dates
2 dried apricots
¾ cup plain yogurt with
   live bacteria

Whiz all the ingredients in a blender until smooth and drink immediately.

banana, avocado & soy smoothie

NUTRIENTS
Vitamins A, B1, B2, B3, B5, B6, C, E, K, beta-carotene, biotin, folate; calcium, chromium, copper, iron, magnesium, manganese, phosphorus, potassium, selenium, zinc; omega-6 fatty acids; tryptophan

If stress keeps you awake at night, try this velvety smoothie packed with sleep-promoting nutrients.

Tryptophan, an amino acid found in bananas, avocados, and soy products, is converted by the brain into serotonin, which has mood-steadying, sleep-inducing properties. The conversion works best if magnesium and vitamins B6 and B3 are also present. This recipe contains all three of these nutrients.

Banana Rich in tryptophan and high in magnesium, which supports the adrenal glands to control the effects of stress, bananas also contain vitamin B6—a key antistress nutrient.

RECIPE

1 ripe banana, peeled
1 avocado, peeled and
   pitted
1¾ cups soymilk
1 tbsp. sunflower seeds

Whiz together the banana, avocado and soymilk in a blender until smooth. Sprinkle the sunflower seeds over and drink immediately.

Avocado This fruit contains a host of B vitamins to promote a good night's sleep as well as high levels of antioxidant vitamin E, which disarm free radicals produced under pressure.

Soymilk Another source of tryptophan, soymilk is a good alternative to cow's milk for anyone who is lactose-intolerant. All soy products have the ability to lower blood-cholesterol levels, helping to protect the heart.

Sunflower Seeds As well as containing tryptophan, sunflower seeds are rich in zinc, a mineral that is depleted in the body by stress. They are also packed with stress-busting vitamin E, which discourages the build up of plaque on artery walls and the formation of blood clots linked to heart disease.

PREPARATION TIPS

• Speed up the ripening of a green banana by placing it in a brown paper bag with an apple.

• A perfectly ripe, ready-to-eat avocado does not have dark sunken spots or cracks, but yields slightly under the thumb.

• Soymilk does not naturally contain calcium so look for a calcium-enriched brand.

• Because of their high fat content, sunflower seeds are prone to rancidity. Store them in an airtight container in the refrigerator.

Use oat or rice milk as other nondairy alternatives to soymilk.

banana, coconut milk & lemon grass smoothie

NUTRIENTS
Vitamins A, B3, B6, C, K, folate; calcium, chromium, iron, magnesium, manganese, phosphorus, potassium, selenium, sodium, zinc; tryptophan

A juice to reduce stress-related high blood pressure.

Bananas are high in potassium, which helps to maintain normal blood pressure and a healthy heart, two conditions often related to stress. Rich in calcium and magnesium, coconut milk supports the adrenal glands. Lemon grass contains manganese, which keeps the nervous system healthy and helps to keep stress at bay.

Use frozen bananas in this recipe for an icy-cool twist.

RECIPE

2 ripe bananas, peeled and chopped
2 cups coconut milk
1 stalk lemon grass (outer leaves removed), chopped into chunks

Whiz the bananas, coconut milk and lemon grass in a blender until smooth. Stir and drink immediately.

tomato, carrot & rosemary

This nutritious juice supports the immune system and heart, both of which can be affected by stress.

Tomatoes are full of vitamin C, which is crucial for iron and calcium absorption—two minerals linked to a healthy nervous system. Both tomatoes and carrots provide large amounts of beta-carotene, which the body converts into vitamin A, a powerful antioxidant that plays a vital role in immune response, and is particularly important when stress hormones are circulating in the system. Rosemary, a fragrant and potent herb, is known for its circulation-boosting and blood capillary-strengthening abilities, which are key to a healthy heart.

NUTRIENTS

Vitamins B1, B2, B3, B5; B6, C, E, K, beta-carotene, folate; calcium, chromium, copper, iron, magnesium, manganese, phosphorus, potassium, sodium; lycopene; tryptophan

RECIPE

a handful fresh rosemary
   sprigs
4 large tomatoes, cut
   into wedges
3 large carrots, topped, tailed,
   and chopped into chunks

Press alternate chunks of tomato and carrot, and the rosemary leaves through a juicer. Stir and drink immediately.

carrot, celery root & beet

NUTRIENTS
Vitamins B6, C, K, beta-carotene, biotin, folate; calcium, chromium, iron, magnesium, manganese, phosphorus, potassium, sodium

This juice helps to offset the damaging effects stress can have on the immune system.

The high levels of beta-carotene in the carrots can help to protect the body from oxidative stress and the dampening effect that long-term stress has on the immune system. Celery root reduces high blood pressure and is rich in calcium and vitamins C and B6, and hence a great tonic for the nervous system. Particularly rich in folate, beets are one of the best vegetables to help stimulate a feeling of well-being.

You can add a squeeze of lemon to this juice to soften the strong taste of the celery root.

RECIPE

4 large carrots, topped, tailed, and chopped into chunks
1 celery root, peeled and chopped into chunks
2 small beets, chopped into chunks

Press alternate chunks of vegetable through a juicer, stir, and drink immediately.

zucchini, lettuce & parsley

This combination promotes relaxation and is a good bedtime choice for insomniacs.

Also known as courgettes and summer squash, zucchini contain folate, which helps to control a chemical process in the brain that turns one type of neurotransmitter into another, creating a feeling of calm. Along with parsley, zucchinis are a good source of vitamin B1, helping to strengthen the nervous system and lower stress levels. Lettuce contains lactones—natural calming opiates, which were used by the ancient Assyrians as a mild sedative. The ancient Greeks believed lettuce induced sleep and served it at the end of a meal. The darker-leaved varieties in particular are a good source of chlorophyll, which helps to keep the blood healthy, reducing the risk of heart disease.

NUTRIENTS
Vitamins B1, B2, B3, C, D, E, beta-carotene, folate; calcium, iodine, iron, magnesium, manganese, phosphorus, potassium, selenium, sodium, zinc; chlorophyll

RECIPE

a handful fresh
 parsley sprigs
½ head of lettuce,
 separated into leaves
3 large zucchini,
 chopped into chunks

Wrap the lettuce leaves around chunks of zucchini and sprigs of parsley. Press alternate ingredients through a juicer, stir, and drink immediately.

cucumber, watercress & licorice

NUTRIENTS
Vitamins A, B3, B5, C, E,
beta-carotene, biotin, folate;
calcium, chromium, iodine,
iron, magnesium, manganese,
phosphorus, potassium, silica,
zinc; lecithin; tryptophan

RECIPE

1 large bunch watercress
1 cucumber, chopped
  into chunks
1 large knob (1½ in.) licorice
  root, chopped
  into chunks

Wrap the watercress leaves
around chunks of cucumber
and licorice root, press through
a juicer, stir, and
drink immediately.

Chill out with this calming and refreshing juice.

The inner temperature of a cucumber can be up to 20°F cooler
than the outside air, so this juice is literally cooling during times
of tension. Watercress is an excellent source of the antioxidant
vitamins A, C, and E, which help to protect the body from stress-
related free-radical damage. A traditional stress-buster, licorice
provides important nutrients for the adrenal glands, helping to
build, strengthen, and relax muscles.

avocado, broccoli & bok choy

This creamy green juice can help to lower blood cholesterol, which is often caused by stress.

Avocados contain lots of potassium, a mineral vital for muscle and nerve function, and oleic acid, a monounsaturated fat that might help to lower cholesterol. A good plant source of calcium, broccoli helps to induce muscle relaxation. Bok choy is a leafy green Chinese vegetable belonging to the cabbage family that has a mild, mustardy taste. Both the leaves and stem can be juiced. Loaded with the antioxidant beta-carotene, bok choy also helps the body to deal with stress hormones.

NUTRIENTS
Vitamins B1, B2, B3, B5, B6, C, E, K, beta-carotene, folate; calcium, copper, iron, magnesium, manganese, phosphorus, potassium, sodium, zinc; tryptophan

Give this juice a spicy kick by adding a dash of hot pepper sauce.

RECIPE

3 broccoli flowerets, chopped into chunks
1 bok choy, quartered lengthways
1 avocado, peeled and pitted

Press alternate chunks of broccoli and bok choy through a juicer. Whiz broccoli and bok choy juice together with the avocado in a blender until smooth. Drink immediately.

apple, black currant & açai berry

NUTRIENTS
Vitamins B1, B2, B3, C, E, K, beta-carotene, folate; calcium, copper, iron, magnesium, phosphorus, potassium, zinc; anthocyanins; omega-3, omega-6, and omega-9 fatty acids; pectin

This juice is packed with age-defying nutrients.

Apples and black currants are rich in vitamin C, which promotes collagen production—essential for smooth-looking skin. Hailed as a "superberry," the chocolatey-tasting açai berry comes from the Brazilian rainforest. Sold as juice or frozen pulp, it boasts omega-3, -6, and -9 fatty acids, which are great for the skin, and a high level of the antioxidant anthocyanin.

RECIPE

4 apples, cut into wedges
40 black currants
1 tbsp. store-bought açai berry juice or defrosted frozen pulp

Press alternate apple chunks, and the black currants through a juicer. Stir in the açai berry juice or pulp and drink immediately.

grapefruit & pomegranate crush

Served over crushed ice, this sweet and sour skin-saving duo is particularly thirst-quenching.

Grapefruit juice contains bioflavonoids, which help the body to absorb vitamin C, important for skin health. A pomegranate provides a good amount of an adult's recommended daily intake of vitamin C, and also supplies natural estrogens to help balance hormones and prevent premature aging. Pomegranate juice is loaded with antioxidants, which work primarily in the skin and help to boost the protective abilities of sunscreens.

NUTRIENTS

Vitamins B3, C, E, beta-carotene, folate; iron, potassium, bioflavonoids; lycopene; pectin

Ruby grapefruits contain more of the potent antioxidant lycopene than golden–yellow varieties.

RECIPE

2 grapefruit, peeled and torn into segments

1¼ cups filtered water, frozen as icecubes

2 pomegranates, cut in half

Press the grapefruit segments through a juicer. Crush the ice in a blender and add the juice. Tap the pomegranate on the skin side with a wooden spoon to remove the seeds, add to the grapefruit juice and ice. Stir and drink immediately.

053

strawberry, cherry & passion fruit

NUTRIENTS
Vitamins B2, B3, B5, B6, C, K, beta-carotene, folate; calcium, copper, iodine, magnesium, manganese, phosphorus, potassium, sodium; bioflavonoids; polyphenols

Packed with powerful, collagen-building nutrients.

Strawberries are one of the highest sources of polyphenols, antioxidants associated with skin health. They also protect the skin's elasticity by supporting collagen production and helping skin to stay wrinklefree. Cherries contain ahuge concentration of antioxidants, which have a powerful protective and regenerative effect on collagen. The passion fruit seeds and flesh add texture, fiber and vitamin C—to promote youthful skin.

RECIPE

25 strawberries, hulled
25 cherries, pitted
2 passion fruit, cut in half

Press alternate strawberries and cherries through a juicer. Scoop out the passion fruit flesh and seeds and add to the juice. Stir and drink immediately.

orange, nectarine & lime

This refreshing juice is fantastically good for rehydrating parched skin.

Oranges are a superb source of vitamin C, a lack of which has been linked to collagen degeneration of the skin and premature aging. Nectarines are an excellent provider of potassium, a mineral essential for the proper functioning of cellular enzymes. Research suggests flavonoids found in limes might protect against skin damage caused by UV rays: many of the flavonoids are found in the white pith, so leave as much on as possible when peeling the lime to insure some goes into your juice.

NUTRIENTS
Vitamins B1, B3, B5, C, beta-carotene, folate; calcium, magnesium, phosphorus, potassium; bioflavonoids; limonin

RECIPE

3 oranges, peeled and torn into segments
2 nectarines, pitted and quartered
1 lime, peeled and quartered

Press alternate chunks of fruit through a juicer, stir, and drink immediately.

A nectarine tree may occasionally produce a branch that bears peaches, and viceversa.

orange, papaya & plum

NUTRIENTS
Vitamins B1, B2, B3, B5, C, E, beta-carotene, folate; calcium, iron, phosphorus, potassium, silicon, sodium; papain

Banish aging under-eye bags and blemishes with this toxin-flushing, skin-clearing juice.

Oranges are a key youth-promoting food, as they are so high in vitamin C. Without this nutrient, skin elasticity collapses, leading to sagging and wrinkles. Papaya, also called pawpaws, is another excellent source of vitamin C. Many skin disorders can be traced to imbalances in the digestive tract, and papaya is important for skin health because it contains papain, an enzyme that helps to digest proteins and stimulate a sluggish digestive system. Plums are iron-rich, promoting healthy, glowing skin.

RECIPE

3 oranges, peeled and torn into segments
1 papaya, peeled, seeded and chopped into chunks
6 plums, pitted and halved

Press alternate chunks of fruit through a juicer, stir, and drink immediately.

cranberry, goji berry & yogurt smoothie

This blend is the ultimate "stop-the-clock" breakfast.

The vitamin C in the cranberries works with the calcium in the yogurt to help the body make collagen and maintain healthy skin. Also known as wolfberries, goji berries grow in the Himalayas and are sold in the West in pure juice form, as they are too fragile to be transported whole. They are an extremely nutrient-dense fruit packed with 18 amino acids, 21 trace minerals and a huge hit of vitamin C.

NUTRIENTS

Vitamins A, B1, B2, B5, B6, B12, C, D, E, beta-carotene; calcium, copper, iodine, iron, manganese, phosphorus, potassium, selenium, zinc; amino acids

RECIPE

40 cranberries
2 cups plain yogurt with live
    bacteria
1 tbsp. store-bought goji
    berry juice

Whiz together the cranberries, goji berry juice and yogurt in a blender until smooth and drink immediately.

If you take blood-thinning medication, avoid cranberry juice because it can cause a toxic reaction.

melon, raspberry & peppermint

NUTRIENTS
Vitamins B1, B2, B3, B6, C, beta-carotene, folate; calcium, chromium, copper, iron, magnesium, manganese, phosphorus, potassium, selenium, sodium

A tasty treat that will make your skin glow.

Thanks to the melon's high water content, this juice is particularly nourishing and cleansing for the skin. Raspberries boast almost 50 percent higher antioxidant activity than strawberries, three times that of kiwi fruit, and ten times the antioxidant activity of tomatoes. Their vitamin C and flavonoid content will also boost the skin's microcirculation, which helps to flush away impurities and leave a rosy glow. Peppermint is a good source of vitamin B3, which is also essential for proper circulation and healthy skin. For maximum nutritional benefit, drink this juice on an empty stomach and then wait 15 minutes before eating.

RECIPE

a handful fresh peppermint leaves
25 raspberries
1 melon, peeled, seeded and chopped into chunks

Wrap the peppermint leaves around the raspberries. Press through a juicer, alternating with chunks of melon. Stir and drink immediately.

pineapple, orange & coconut

Soothe blotchy and inflamed skin with this flavorful complexion-calming trio.

Pineapple is extremely rich in vitamin C and bromelain, an enzyme that has anti-inflammatory properties to help encourage smooth, blotch-free skin. Oranges also contain vitamin C, which reduces the speed at which the skin ages. Deliciously sweet in flavor, coconut is a good source of zinc, found in every cell of the body and known to stimulate hair growth. Coconut also contains lauric acid, which has been shown to plump up wrinkles and soothe irritated skin.

NUTRIENTS

Vitamins B1, B2, B3, B5, B6, C, K, beta-carotene, folate; calcium, copper, iron, magnesium, manganese, phosphorus, potassium, selenium, sodium, zinc; bromelain

RECIPE

1 pineapple, peeled and
   chopped into chunks
2 oranges, peeled and torn
   into segments
1 fresh coconut, broken in half
   and white flesh scraped out

Press alternate chunks of
fruit through a juicer, stir,
and drink immediately.

apple, carrot & evening primrose oil

NUTRIENTS
Vitamins C, E, K, beta-carotene, folate; calcium, chromium, iron, magnesium, omega-6 fatty acids, phosphorus, potassium; gamma-linoleic acid; pectin

A delicious and effective internal moisturizer.

Vitamin C in the apple helps the body to form collagen, the connective tissue that keeps skin firm. The carrot's beta-carotene enhances the activity of essential fatty acids, particularly gamma-linoleic acid (GLA), which is present in the evening primrose oil and is important for skin health. Omega-6 fatty acids are vital for healthy cell regeneration and keeping skin well-nourished and wrinkle free. Evening primrose oil is also rich in skin-enhancing vitamin E.

RECIPE

4 apples, cut into wedges
3 large carrots, topped, tailed, and chopped into chunks
1 tbsp. evening primrose oil

Press alternate chunks of apple and carrot through a juicer. Stir in the evening primrose oil and drink immediately.

tofu, blueberry & hempseed oil smoothie

This smoothie is loaded with antiaging nutrients.

Tofu is rich in protein, the raw material that is needed to build collagen, which minimizes wrinkles and gives you younger-looking skin, while blueberries contain anthocyanins, antioxidants that neutralize free-radical damage to the skin. A true superfood, hempseed oil is packed with nutrients: it contains 21 minerals, 13 vitamins, eight amino acids, and two essential fatty acids, all of which play a key role in maintaining muscle tone and glowing skin.

NUTRIENTS
Vitamins A, C, E, K, beta-carotene; calcium, copper, iron, magnesium, manganese, phosphorus, potassium, selenium, sulfur, zinc; amino acids; anthocyanins; chlorophyll; gamma-linoleic acid; omega-3 and omega-6 fatty acids; tryptophan

RECIPE

400g/14 oz silken tofu
40 blueberries
1 tbsp hempseed oil

Whiz together the tofu and blueberries in a blender until smooth. Stir in the hempseed oil and drink immediately.

80 percent of hempseed oil is made up of essential fatty acids.

carrot, cucumber, olive & basil

NUTRIENTS

Vitamins B1, B2, C, D, E, K, beta-carotene, folate; calcium, chromium, copper, iron, magnesium, manganese, phosphorus, potassium, silica; omega-3 and omega-6 essential fatty acids; tryptophan

Tasty and nourishing, this drink provides a huge cell-rejuvenating dose of nutrients.

Research shows that diet and lifestyle greatly affect the quality of skin. Toxins, sugary foods, saturated fats, cigarette smoke, traffic pollution, and excessive sun exposure can lead to clogged pores and premature aging. Yet the right nutrients can help to halt, and even reverse this damage.

Carrot This vegetable is best known for its star nutrient beta-carotene, which is easily digestible in juice. Beta-carotene slows the aging process by helping to keep skin clear and healthy.

> Studies show that the essential oil in basil leaves has a powerful antibacterial action.

RECIPE

a handful fresh basil leaves
10 olives, pitted
3 large carrots, topped, tailed, and chopped into chunks
½ cucumber, chopped into chunks

Wrap the basil leaves around the olives and chunks of carrot and cucumber. Press chunks of vegetable and olives through a juicer, stir, and drink immediately.

Cucumber A superb source of silica, cucumber is often recommended to improve the complexion. Silica is an essential component of healthy connective tissue. Cucumber's high water content makes it naturally hydrating—a must for glowing skin.

Olive Collagen, the "glue" that holds muscle tissue together, requires the presence of copper, and olives are a good source of this trace mineral. They also contain vitamin E, which is known to prolong cell life and to help to treat skin problems, such as eczema, sunburn, and stretch marks.

Basil This herb is rich in manganese, needed for healthy skin, bone, and cartilage. Traditionally, basil was prescribed to stimulate blood flow, helping to revive the skin's youthful glow.

PREPARATION TIPS

- If you buy carrots with their green tops attached, remove them before storage as they tend to draw moisture from the roots and cause the carrots to wilt.

- Store carrots away from apples, pears, potatoes, and other fruits and vegetables that produce ethylene gas, as it makes them taste bitter.

- Leave the peel on unwaxed cucumbers, but peel waxed ones. Unwaxed cucumbers lose moisture easily, so keep them wrapped tightly in plastic wrap.

- To pit olives, press them with the flat side of a knife, then break the flesh and remove the pit with your fingers.

carrot, asparagus & lemon grass

NUTRIENTS
Vitamins B1, B2, B3, B6, C, E, K; beta-carotene, folate; calcium, chromium, copper, iron, magnesium, manganese, phosphorus, potassium, selenium, sodium, zinc; tryptophan

This juice is loaded with skin-replenishing nutrients.

The antioxidant properties of carrots are vital for healthy blood cells and beautiful skin. Asparagus is a rare vegetable source of youth-enhancing vitamin E. A popular ingredient in Thai cuisine, lemon grass is also used in many preparations to treat conditions such as acne and cellulite. As part of a drink, it aids lymphatic detoxification, strengthens connective tissue, and helps to tighten the skin.

For speed, use scissors to trim the woody ends off asparagus spears.

RECIPE

4 large carrots, topped, tailed, and chopped into chunks
10 asparagus spears, chopped into chunks
1 stalk lemon grass (outer leaves removed), chopped

Press alternate chunks of ingredients through a juicer, stir, and drink immediately.

063

avocado & soy yogurt smoothie

A nutritious internal skin booster, this smoothie also makes a great skin-smoothing face pack.

Avocados are a rich source of monounsaturated fatty acids including oleic acid and vitamin E—wonderful skin hydrators. They also contain natural chemicals that stimulate the production of collagen, which is the body's first defense against wrinkles. Soymilk also contains vitamin E and magnesium, essential to repair cells and tissues. Dark purple nori is the most digestible seaweed and contains a wealth of nutrients to nourish and protect the skin so it stays firm and smooth.

NUTRIENTS

Vitamins A, B1, B2, B3, B5, B6, C, D, E, K, beta-carotene, biotin, folate; calcium, copper, iodine, iron, magnesium, manganese, phosphorus, potassium, sodium, zinc; lignans; omega-6 fatty acids; tryptophan

RECIPE

1 avocado, peeled and
   pitted
1¼ cups soy yogurt
1 tbsp. nori flakes

Blend the avocado and yogurt until smooth. Sprinkle the nori over and drink immediately.

apple, cherry & fig

NUTRIENTS
Vitamins C, K, beta-carotene; calcium, magnesium, manganese, phosphorus, potassium; bioflavonoids; malic acid; pectin; tryptophan

Suitable for sensitive stomachs, this juice helps to stimulate a sluggish digestive system.

A ripe, raw apple is one of the easiest foods for the stomach to digest, especially in its juice form. The pectin contained in the apple helps to encourage the growth of beneficial bacteria in the gut, working like roughage to encourage movement, but interestingly, it also helps to treat diarrhea. Cherries are naturally antispasmodic and have anti-inflammatory properties, which help to bring relief to sufferers of irritable bowel syndrome (IBS), as well as arthritis. The figs contain ficin, a useful, protein-breaking enzyme with laxative effects.

RECIPE

4 apples, cut into wedges
25 cherries, pitted
2 figs, stems removed

Press alternate chunks of fruit through a juicer, stir, and drink immediately.

065

papaya, apricot & blueberry

This potent, sweet-tasting juice is overflowing with digestion-friendly nutrients.

Papaya contains the enzyme papain, which helps to digest the protein in food. A natural laxative, apricot juice helps to promote bowel movement. Both papaya and apricot are also rich in salicylate, a natural compound with pain-relieving properties. Blueberries are high in pectin, a soluble fiber, which helps to lower cholesterol and prevent bile acid from being transformed into a potentially cancer-causing form in the colon.

NUTRIENTS

Vitamins B2, B3, B5, C, E; beta-carotene, folate; calcium, iodine, iron, magnesium, manganese, phosphorus, potassium, silicon, sodium, zinc; papain; pectin; tryptophan

Papaya can help to restore the friendly bacteria in the gut after a course of antibiotics.

RECIPE

1 papaya, peeled, seeded and chopped into chunks
4 apricots, halved and pitted
40 blueberries

Press alternate chunks of fruit, and the berries through a juicer. Stir and drink immediately.

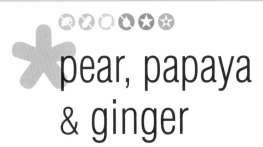

pear, papaya & ginger

NUTRIENTS
Vitamins B6, C, E, folate; beta-carotene; calcium, copper, iodine, iron, magnesium, manganese, phosphorus, potassium, silicon, sodium, zinc; papain; pectin

RECIPE

3 large ripe pears, chopped into chunks
1 papaya, peeled, seeded and chopped into chunks
1 large knob (1½ in.) fresh gingerroot, peeled and cut into chunks

Press alternate chunks of pear and papaya and grated ginger through a juicer. Stir and drink immediately.

Packed with important enzymes and fiber, this tasty trio is deeply cleansing for the digestive system.

Fresh fruit and raw vegetables all contain digestive enzymes, which reduce the digestive load on the body. Raw juices are particularly beneficial because the enzymes are in a form that the body can easily digest.

Pear This fruit contains lots of the soluble fiber pectin, which binds to carcinogenic chemicals in the colon, preventing them from damaging colon cells. Pears are also a good source of the trace mineral copper, a lack of which has been linked to an increased risk of colon cancer. Research shows that pears are considered to be the least allergenic of all foods.

Papaya Rich in fiber, which helps to flush out toxins, papaya is useful for sufferers of irritable bowel syndrome (IBS). This fruit is also loaded with several unique protein-digesting enzymes, including papain and chymopapain, which boost the digestive process. According to studies these enzymes also help to reduce inflammation and enable the body to absorb an increased level of nutrients from food.

Gingerroot The root of the ginger plant is widely used as a digestive aid for mild stomach upsets and is commonly recommended by professional herbalists to help prevent or treat nausea and vomiting associated with motion sickness. Several studies have found ginger is more effective than a placebo in relieving the nausea and vomiting experienced during the early stages of pregnancy.

PREPARATION TIPS

• Pears ripen from the inside out. To tell whether a pear is ripe, apply gentle thumb pressure near the base of the stem. If it yields slightly, it's ripe.

• The juice from pears will be clearer if they are stored in the refrigerator.

• Although the flesh of a papaya is completely free from toxins, tiny amounts of carpine, a toxic substance that's said to depress the nervous system, is found in the black seeds, so always remove them before juicing.

• Choose fresh gingerroot rather than dried, as it tastes better and contains higher levels of gingerol, its anti-inflammatory compound.

The ancient Greeks used ginger for digestive problems and as an antidote to poisoning.

banana, frozen yogurt & ginger smoothie

NUTRIENTS
Vitamins A, B2, B5, B6, B12, C, D, K, beta-carotene, folate; calcium, chromium, copper, iodine, iron, magnesium, manganese, phosphorus, potassium, sodium, zinc; tryptophan

This stomach settler can prevent travel sickness.

Bananas make this smoothie a filling as well as nutritious drink. They also contain a type of fiber, fructoliogosaccharides, which coupled with the acidophilus in the yogurt, encourages the growth of friendly bacteria in the gut. Bananas have also been shown to help protect the stomach from excess hydrochloric acid, linked to indigestion, heartburn and stomach pain. Ginger absorbs and neutralizes toxins in the stomach and also stimulates the circulation, which can help in the prevention of travel sickness and nausea.

RECIPE

2 ripe bananas, peeled
1¾ cups plain yogurt with live bacteria, frozen
1 small knob (¾ in.) fresh gingerroot, peeled and finely grated

Whiz together the bananas, yogurt, and ginger in a blender until smooth. Eat immediately with a spoon or wait 10 minutes and drink.

For an extra special treat, swap the frozen yogurt with vanilla ice cream.

black currant, banana & yogurt smoothie

Soothes an irritable bowel and tastes great.

A handful of black currants contain a good amount of the recommended daily fiber intake—vital for good digestive health. Compounds in bananas help to activate an antacid effect in the stomach. Organic bio-yogurt is loaded with acidophilus, a beneficial bacteria found in the intestines. A good source of essential fatty acids, pumpkin seeds calm an irritated gut.

NUTRIENTS
Vitamins A, B1, B2, B3, B5, B12, C, D, E, beta-carotene, folate; calcium, iodine, iron, magnesium, manganese, phosphorus, potassium, selenium, zinc; omega-3 and omega-6 fatty acids

RECIPE

25 black currants
1 ripe banana, peeled
1¾ cups plain yogurt with
  live bacteria
1 tbsp. pumpkin seeds

Whiz together the berries, banana, and yogurt in a blender until smooth. Sprinkle the pumpkin seeds over and drink immediately.

cucumber, celery & kiwi fruit

NUTRIENTS
Vitamins B1, B2, B6, C, E,
beta-carotene, folate;
calcium, copper, iron,
magnesium, manganese,
phosphorus, potassium,
selenium, silica; tryptophan

Calm all kinds of digestive disruption with this
mouthwatering combination.

The alkalizing properties of cucumber juice help to neutralize
acid in the gut and soothe abdominal pain linked to excess
gas. Studies show it can also dissolve the uric acid that causes
kidney and bladder stones. Celery aids digestion and prevents
bloat-causing fermentation in the gut, while kiwi fruit are an
excellent source of digestive enzymes, enabling the body to top
up its supplies, which can become depleted by factors such as
poor diet, age, lack of mobility, and some medication.

RECIPE

**1 cucumber, chopped
into chunks
4 celery stalks including
tops, chopped into chunks
2 kiwi fruit, chopped
into chunks**

Press alternate chunks of
cucumber, celery, and kiwi
fruit through a juicer, stir,
and drink immediately.

mango, pear & aloe vera

Drink this stomach-soothing juice just before a meal to create the ideal conditions for healthy digestion.

Mango contains an enzyme with stomach-settling properties and helps to combat acidity and poor digestion. A good source of the soluble fiber pectin, pear stimulates a sluggish digestive system. Used as a healing remedy for centuries, aloe vera juice has been found to contain 20 minerals, 18 amino acids, and 12 vitamins. Thanks to its ability to encourage the release of pepsin, a gastric enzyme necessary for digestion, aloe vera also helps to ease constipation and prevent diarrhea.

NUTRIENTS
Vitamins B1, B2, B3, B6, C, E, beta-carotene, folate; calcium, copper, iron, magnesium, manganese, phosphorus, potassium, zinc; amino acids; pectin

RECIPE

1 mango, peeled, pitted
   and chopped into chunks
3 large ripe pears, chopped
   into chunks
1 tbsp. store-bought aloe
   vera juice

Press alternate chunks of fruit through a juicer. Stir in the aloe vera juice and drink immediately.

Aloe vera has been shown to be an effective treatment for frostbite.

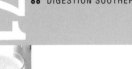

apple, lemon & fennel

Drink this juice after lunch or dinner to help with digesting a heavy meal.

The malic and tartaric acid content of apples help to settle digestion, while the lemon juice has a cleansing effect on the liver. Lemon also induces the production of bile, which helps to flush out the bile duct. This is particularly beneficial after a bout of excessive eating and/or drinking. Historically, fennel has been used to relieve intestinal spasms, cramps, and wind. It is the volatile oils that give fennel its unique aniseedy flavor and digestive properties.

NUTRIENTS

Vitamins C, K, beta-carotene, folate; calcium, chromium, cobalt, iron, magnesium, manganese, phosphorus, potassium, selenium, silicon, sodium, zinc; bioflavonoids; limonin; malic acid; pectin; tartaric acid

RECIPE

4 apples, cut into wedges
2 lemons, peeled and
quartered
1 fennel bulb, quartered

Press alternate ingredients through a juicer, stir, and drink immediately.

pineapple, lime & sweet potato

This delicious, vibrant juice will help to calm inflammation in the digestive tract.

Pineapple juice contains bromelain, a protein-digesting enzyme, which encourages the excretion of hydrochloric acid and insures the maximum absorption of nutrients from the lime and sweet potato. Lime juice is alkalizing, helping to ease heartburn and bloating, as well as cleanse and stimulate the liver and kidneys. Sweet potatoes are renowned for their ability to calm inflammation, soothe ulcers, and boost circulation.

NUTRIENTS

Vitamins B1, B2, B6, C, E, beta-carotene, folate; calcium, copper, iron, magnesium, manganese, phosphorus, potassium; bioflavonoids; bromelain; limonin

RECIPE

**1 pineapple, peeled and
 chopped into chunks**
1 lime, peeled and quartered
**1 sweet potato, chopped
 into chunks**

Press alternate chunks of pineapple, lime, and sweet potato through a juicer, stir, and drink immediately.

A pineapple is ready for juicing when it feels heavy and smells sweet.

cabbage, carrot & fennel

NUTRIENTS
Vitamins B1, B2, B6, C, E, K, beta-carotene, folate; calcium, chromium, cobalt, iodine, iron, magnesium, manganese, phosphorus, potassium, selenium, silicon, sodium, zinc

This juice is a powerful healing remedy, which helps to soothe stomach ulcers.

Traditionally, raw cabbage juice has been prescribed for a number of gastric complaints, including stomach ulcers, intestinal wind, and bloating. Don't drink huge amounts at one time though, as too much cabbage juice can actually cause bloating, as well as cramping. The antioxidant properties of the beta-carotene in the carrots help to mop up toxins produced by slow-moving digestion and bacterial infections. Fennel has a strong calmative and anti-inflammatory action.

RECIPE

¼ medium cabbage, chopped into chunks
3 large carrots, topped, tailed, and chopped into chunks
2 fennel bulbs, quartered

Press alternate chunks of cabbage, carrot, and fennel through a juicer, stir, and drink immediately.

zucchini, cucumber & peppermint

A refreshing concoction to calm an acid stomach, this combination is best served over ice.

This blend of juices is rich in the organic alkalizing elements potassium and phosphorus, which help to neutralize stomach acidity, expel gas and kick-start a sluggish digestive system. Zucchini and cucumbers boast cooling, and anti-spasmodic properties, while the natural oils in peppermint are soothing and gently laxative.

NUTRIENTS
Vitamins B1, B2, B3, C, beta-carotene, folate; calcium, iron, magnesium, manganese, phosphorus, potassium, selenium, silica, sodium, zinc; tryptophan

RECIPE

a handful fresh
   peppermint leaves
2 zucchini, chopped
   into chunks
1 cucumber, chopped
   into chunks

Wrap the peppermint leaves around chunks of zucchini and cucumber and press through a juicer. Stir and drink immediately.

Turn this juice into the perfect cocktail for a hot summer's evening by adding a shot of vodka.

075

apple, cranberry & plum

NUTRIENTS
Vitamins B2, C, K, beta-carotene; calcium, iron, magnesium, manganese, phosphorus, potassium; bioflavonoids; malic acid; pectin

All three of the fruits in this delicious combination contain vital, cell-protecting flavonoids.

Apples are an excellent source of the flavonoid quercetin, thought to be a potent antioxidant that counteracts the damaging effects of free radicals. Phytochemical powerhouses, cranberries are also packed with antioxidants, as well as manganese, a trace mineral that helps to activate superoxide dismutase—an important antioxidant enzyme. Plums are loaded with antiviral, antibacterial vitamin C, which is crucial to the optimal function of a healthy immune system.

RECIPE

4 apples, cut into wedges
4 plums, pitted and halved
40 cranberries

Press alternate chunks of apple and plum, and the cranberries through a juicer. Stir and drink immediately.

cherry, peach & blackberry

Try this mouth-tingling, immunity-boosting cocktail at the first sign of an infection.

Cherries house significant levels of melatonin, an antioxidant that fights off toxins believed to cause or worsen many diseases. They also contain perillyl alcohol, a natural ingredient that's been linked to a reduced risk of cancer. Bursting with antioxidant vitamin C, peaches ideal for juicing are firm and colorful, but avoid any tinged with green as they will never ripen properly. Blackberries pack a powerful nutritional punch, containing high levels of vitamin C and several disease-busting compounds, including ellagic acid.

NUTRIENTS
Vitamins C, E, beta-carotene, folate; calcium, iron, magnesium, phosphorus, potassium, selenium, zinc; bioflavonoids; ellagic acid; melatonin

After juicing blackberries, freeze the pulp in ice-cube trays and use this to flavour drinking water.

RECIPE

2 peaches, pitted and
   quartered
25 cherries, pitted
25 blackberries

Press alternate ingredients through a juicer, stir, and drink immediately.

kiwi fruit, strawberry & grape

NUTRIENTS
Vitamins B1, B2, B3, B5, B6, C, E, K, beta-carotene, biotin, folate; copper, iodine, magnesium, manganese, potassium, zinc; bioflavonoids; ellagic acid; flavones; lutein; tannins

Dose up on vitamin C with this fruity treat.

All three fruits in this juice provide a massive infection-fighting boost of vitamin C and can help to shorten the duration of a cold. The kiwi fruit also contain lutein, a phytonutrient known to reduce the risk of cancer, heart disease, and eye disease. Both strawberries and grapes are high in ellagic acid, which neutralizes carcinogens. The tannins, flavones, and active compounds in the grapes combine to make them energizing and strengthen the cell walls of blood vessels.

RECIPE

3 kiwi fruit, chopped into chunks
15 strawberries, hulled
25 seedless grapes

Press alternate chunks of kiwi fruit, the strawberries and the grapes through a juicer. Stir and drink immediately.

tangerine, mango, papaya & pomegranate

This exotic juice is a mighty immunity-booster.

Rich in vitamin C from tangerines, this tasty juice also contains mango and papaya, which are excellent sources of immunity-boosting beta-carotene and vitamin E. Beta-carotene is known to reduce the risk of stomach cancer when combined with other antioxidants. Pomegranates have been eaten for centuries for their anti-inflammatory properties and they contain natural estrogens, which might also have anticarcinogenic properties.

NUTRIENTS
Vitamin B3, C, E, beta-carotene, folate; calcium, iron, magnesium, phosphorus, potassium, silicon, sodium

RECIPE

3 tangerines, peeled and torn into segments
1 mango, peeled, pitted and chopped into chunks
1 papaya, peeled, seeded, and chopped into chunks
2 pomegranates, cut in half

Press alternate chunks of tangerine, mango, and papaya through a juicer. Tap the pomegranate on the skin side with a wooden spoon to remove the seeds. Add to the mix, stir, and drink immediately.

watermelon, mango & blueberry

NUTRIENTS
Vitamins B1, B3, B6, C, E, beta-carotene, folate; calcium, iron, magnesium, manganese, potassium; bioflavonoids; lycopene

Rejuvenate the immune system with this tasty juice.

Watermelon consists of about 92 percent water. It also contains beta-carotene, vitamin C, and the antioxidant lycopene, which neutralize free radicals. Mango is rich in cell-protecting vitamins and phytochemicals, while blueberries are abundant in blood-cleansing flavonoids. Make this delicious juice extra special by freezing additional watermelon juice and adding a couple of cubes to each glass.

RECIPE

½ watermelon, peeled and chopped into chunks
1 mango, peeled, pitted and chopped into chunks
20 blueberries

Press alternate chunks of watermelon and mango, and the blueberries through a juicer. Stir and drink immediately.

orange, kiwi fruit, carrot & basil

After a period of ill health, restore immunity with this nourishing juice.

Oranges are well-known for their vitamin C content, but they also provide more than 170 phytochemicals and over 60 flavonoids—all with immunity-boosting benefits. Kiwi fruit is packed with beta-carotene as well as vitamin C, and have been shown to protect DNA from damage. Falcarinol, a phytonutrient found in carrots, is also thought to reduce the risk of cancer. Compounds in basil leaves can inhibit several species of harmful bacteria that have become resistant to common antibiotics.

NUTRIENTS
Vitamins B1, B3, B5, C, E, K, beta-carotene, folate; calcium, chromium, copper, iron, magnesium, manganese, potassium; bioflavonoids; intein

RECIPE

a handful fresh basil leaves
2 oranges, peeled and torn into segments
2 kiwi fruit, chopped into chunks
2 large carrots, topped, tailed, and chopped into chunks

Wrap the basil leaves around orange segments and press through a juicer, alternating with, kiwi fruit, and carrot. Stir and drink immediately.

Kiwi fruit is very high in intein, an antioxidant that protects against eye disease.

berry & yogurt smoothie

NUTRIENTS
Vitamins A, B2, B3, B5, B6, B12, C, D, E, K, beta-carotene, folate; calcium, copper, iodine, iron, magnesium, manganese, phosphorus, potassium, zinc; anthocyanins; bioflavonoids; ellagic acid; ellagitannins

RECIPE

10 strawberries, hulled
25 raspberries
25 blueberries
1¾ cups plain yogurt with live bacteria

Whiz together the berries and yogurt in a blender until smooth, and drink immediately.

This is the perfect breakfast during convalescence, or whenever you can't face solid food.

The super-nutrient vitamin C is needed for more than 300 different processes in the body, but it is easily wiped out by smoking, pollution, and stress. Found in abundance in berries, vitamin C and other antioxidants help to quash the damaging free radicals that are associated with many illnesses.

Strawberry An average serving of strawberries provides more than the daily recommended intake of vitamin C for adults. Strawberries also contain ellagic acid, a phytochemical that is proven to protect against many diseases and helps to destroy some of the toxins in cigarette smoke and polluted air.

Raspberry This soft fruit is rich in ellagitannins, a family of antioxidant compounds, which have anticarcinogenic properties almost exclusive to raspberries. They are also loaded with manganese and vitamin C—two antioxidants that help to protect the body's tissue from oxygen-related damage.

Blueberry Top in the antioxidant league tables, blueberries owe part of their "superberry" status to the powerful phytonutrients anthocyanin and ellagic acid, which are known to help stop cancer in its tracks. They also contain a high level of immunity-boosting vitamin C.

Yogurt Each serving of plain yogurt with live bacteria contains millions of beneficial bacteria, such as lactobacillus, which play a vital role in supporting the immune system.

PREPARATION TIPS

• Leave the stems on strawberries until you are ready to juice them, as this helps to preserve their nutrient content.

• Raspberries are very fragile and must be handled with care to avoid bruising, which will compromise their nutritional content.

• Look for blueberries that have a silvery bloom, which is an indication of freshness. They should also be uniform in size and plump, not shriveled.

• Buy yogurt well before the "use by" date, the older it gets, the less beneficial bacteria it contains. Store it inside the refrigerator, not in the door, because exposure to heat also destroys the friendly bacteria.

The blueberry is one of the few fruits native to North America.

celery, carrot & lemon

The wide range of nutrients in this tangy trio make this juice highly effective at fighting infections.

Celery contains coumarins, compounds that help to prevent free radicals from damaging cells and enhance the activity of immunity-defending white blood cells. Other compounds in celery—acetylenics—inhibit the growth of tumors. Carrots are a very rich source of beta-carotene, while lemons are alkalizing, and have antiseptic qualities, which make them very useful for treating sore throats.

RECIPE

6 celery stalks, including tops,
   chopped into chunks
2 large carrots, topped, tailed,
   and chopped into chunks
2 lemons, peeled and
   quartered

Press alternate chunks of celery, carrot, and lemon through a juicer, stir, and drink immediately.

083

carrot, zucchini & cilantro

These fabulously healthy ingredients make a potent immunity-boosting combination.

More than 200 studies suggest beta-carotene plays a role in cancer prevention, and carrots are the best source of this antioxidant, which neutralizes harmful free radicals. Carrot juice also contains alpha-carotene, another powerful antioxidant. Zucchini add extra beta-carotene and vitamin C, while cilantro contains antibiotic substances that can prevent some forms of food poisoning. For this reason it has been used since ancient times to treat stomach upsets and infections.

NUTRIENTS
Vitamins C, K, alpha-carotene, beta-carotene, folate; calcium, chromium, iron, magnesium, phosphorus, potassium, sodium

RECIPE

a handful of fresh cilantro leaves
4 large carrots, topped, tailed, and chopped into chunks
2 zucchini, chopped into chunks

Wrap the coriander leaves around chunks of carrot and courgette. Press alternate chunks through a juicer. Stir and drink immediately.

When peeling carrots, peel as finely as possible as many nutrients lie close to the skin.

carrot, cauliflower & turmeric

NUTRIENTS
Vitamins B1, B2, B3, B5, B6, C, K, beta-carotene, folate; boron, calcium, chromium, iron, magnesium, manganese, phosphorus, potassium, zinc; curcumin; indoles; tryptophan

This spicy juice has many healing properties.

Carrots are packed with immunity-supporting antioxidants. Cauliflower contains nutrients that help to neutralize cell-damaging substances and prevent tumor growth. Traditionally, curcumin, the active ingredient in turmeric, has been used to treat conditions including toothache, bruises, chest pain, and colic. It also has anti-inflammatory properties and is a powerful antioxidant, protecting against toxins and free radicals.

Always buy cauliflowers with white flowerets, as those with brown specks are past their best.

RECIPE

4 large carrots, topped, tailed, and chopped into chunks
½ small head cauliflower, broken into pieces
½ tsp. turmeric powder

Press alternate chunks of carrot and cauliflower through a juicer, stir in the turmeric powder, and drink immediately.

pepper, onion, garlic & parsley

Medicine in a glass, this juice is bursting with antioxidants and antibacterial agents.

Red and yellow bell peppers contain up to four times the vitamin C in an orange. Onion contains exceptionally high levels of the flavonoid quercertin, which is a powerful antiviral, antibacterial, and anti-inflammatory. When the allicin in the garlic is crushed, it combines with allinase and results in antibacterial action equivalent to one percent penicillin. Parsley is also rich in vitamin C.

NUTRIENTS
Vitamins B1, B2, B3, B6, C, D, E, beta-carotene, folate; calcium, chromium, copper, iron, magnesium, manganese, phosphorus, potassium, selenium, sulfur, zinc; allicin; bioflavonoids; tryptophan

RECIPE

a handful fresh parsley sprigs
2 bell peppers, seeded and
   chopped into chunks
2 onions, peeled and cut
   into wedges
2 cloves garlic, peeled

Wrap the parsley sprigs around chunks of bell pepper and onion. Press alternate chunks, and the garlic through a juicer. Stir and drink immediately.

pepper, tomato, watercress & olive oil

NUTRIENTS
Vitamins B1, B2, B3, B5, B6, C, D, E, K, beta-carotene, folate; calcium, chromium, copper, iodine, iron, magnesium, manganese, phosphorus, potassium; lycopene; omega-3 and omega-6 essential fatty acids; tryptophan

A peppery juice that boosts the immune system.

Peppers are rich in the antioxidants beta-carotene, as well as being rich in vitamin C. The lycopene, a type of caretonoid in the tomatoes, has powerful anticarcinogenic properties, while watercress contains compounds that have been found to mop up damaging free radicals. The antioxidants in olive oil, such as vitamins E and K, provide a defence mechanism that helps to prevent the onset of many diseases.

RECIPE

1 large bunch watercress
1 bell pepper, seeded and chopped into chunks
4 large tomatoes, cut into wedges
1 tbsp. extra virgin olive oil

Wrap the watercress leaves around chunks of bell pepper and tomato. Press vegetables through a juicer. Stir in the olive oil and drink immediately.

tofu, avocado & soymilk smoothie

Loaded with protein and antioxidants, this recipe is a top health-enhancing juice.

The phytoestrogens found in tofu might help to regulate the dominance of estrogen, a contributing factor in hormone-related cancers, such as breast cancer. Avocados contain carotenoids and vitamin E, which inhibit the growth of prostate cancer. Geinstein, a phytochemical in soymilk, is thought to inhibit the growth of small tumors. And pumpkin seeds are full of zinc, which accelerates healing and plays an important role in protecting against infection.

NUTRIENTS

Vitamins A, B1, B2, B3, B5, B6, C, E, K, beta-carotene, biotin, folate; calcium, copper, iron, magnesium, manganese, phosphorus, potassium, selenium, zinc; omega-3 and omega-6 fatty acids; tryptophan

Firmer tofu is usually higher in fat than softer varieties, which are often called silky or silken.

RECIPE

14 oz. silken tofu
1 avocado, peeled and pitted
⅓ cup soymilk
1 tbsp. pumpkin seeds

Whiz together the tofu, avocado and soymilk in a blender until smooth. Sprinkle the pumpkin seeds over and drink immediately.

apple, strawberry & lime

Both the taste and the aroma of this refreshing juice are guaranteed to lift a low mood.

Apples contain calcium and magnesium, which together help to balance brain chemistry. Strawberries are rich in the antioxidant anthocyanins, which might protect the brain's ability to respond to the chemical messengers that control mood. All three ingredients are rich in vitamin C, which aids the synthesis of neurotransmitters in the brain. Recent research shows that just smelling the scent of cinnamon boosts the brain's activity.

NUTRIENTS

Vitamins B2, B3, B5, B6, C, K, beta-carotene, folate; calcium, copper, iodine, magnesium, manganese, phosphorus, potassium; anthocyanins; bioflavonoids; limonin; malic acid; pectin

RECIPE

4 apples, cut into wedges
2 limes, peeled and quartered
15 strawberries, hulled
1 tsp. ground cinnamon

Press alternate chunks of apple and lime, and the strawberries through a juicer. Sprinkle the cinnamon over, stir and drink immediately.

Cinnamon is the bark of the cinnamon tree, dried and rolled into a tubular form, known as a quill.

apple, grape & blueberry

This tangy juice is positively bursting with memory-enhancing nutrients.

The simple sugars in the apples and the B-vitamins in the grapes can help to improve a poor attention span and boost concentration. In studies, researchers have found that blueberries help to protect the brain from oxidative stress and might reduce the effects of age-related memory conditions. Anthocyanin, the formidable antioxidant that gives blueberries their amazing color, also appears to protect the neurons in the brain, which helps to improve balance, coordination, and short-term memory.

NUTRIENTS
Vitamins B1, B3, B6, C, E , K, beta-carotene, biotin; calcium, iron, magnesium, manganese, phosphorus, potassium, selenium, zinc; anthocyanins; malic acid; pectin

RECIPE

4 apples, cut into wedges
25 seedless grapes
25 blueberries

Press alternate chunks of apple, and the grapes and blueberries through a juicer. Stir and drink immediately.

pineapple, banana & coconut smoothie

NUTRIENTS
Vitamins B1, B2, B6, C, K, beta-carotene, folate; calcium, chromium, copper, iron, magnesium, manganese, phosphorus, potassium, selenium, sodium; bromelain; tryptophan

This taste of the Caribbean will lift your spirits.

A lack of manganese, a mineral that is found in pineapple and banana, has been linked to insomnia and restlessness, which can make you feel low. Bananas are rich in slow-releasing carbohydrates, which help to improve concentraton levels. The zinc in coconut milk is essential for good mental health, helping to protect against many conditions, such as depression, anxiety, and anorexia.

RECIPE

1 pineapple, peeled and chopped into chunks
2 ripe bananas, peeled
1¼ cups coconut milk

Whiz together the pineapple, bananas and coconut milk in a blender until smooth and drink immediately.

banana & peanut butter smoothie

Kids will love this protein-rich smoothie that replenishes both mental and physical energy.

The carbohydrates in bananas help to stabilize blood sugar levels, while the potassium makes the brain more alert. Peanut butter contains more than 25 percent protein—important for energy, as well as the plant compound resveratrol, which is thought to protect the brain from degenerative diseases. A fine source of slow-burning energy, milk contains several B-vitamins, including B2, which is important for energy production, and B12, which helps to create red blood cells, improve concentration, and prevent memory loss.

NUTRIENTS

Vitamins A, B2, B3, B6, B12, C, D, E, K, beta-carotene, folate; calcium, chromium, iodine, iron, magnesium, manganese, phosphorus, potassium, selenium, sodium; tryptophan

RECIPE

2 ripe bananas, peeled
1 tbsp. peanut butter
2 cups milk

Whiz together all the ingredients in a blender until smooth and drink immediately.

More than 80 percent of the fat in peanut butter is unsaturated, which is heart-healthy.

mango & soymilk smoothie

Get the day off to a brilliant start with this memory-sharpening breakfast smoothie.

Mango is loaded with beta-carotene and also contains vitamin B3, both of which are known to promote good brain health. The vitamin B6 found in soy is important for the creation of neurotransmitters—the brain's chemical messengers. A low intake of vitamin B6 can result in memory impairment and trouble retaining and retrieving information. Sunflower seeds are a rich source of omega-6 essential fatty acids that are crucial for the brain to function efficiently.

NUTRIENTS

Vitamins B1, B2, B3, B6, C, E, beta-carotene, folate; calcium, copper, iron, magnesium, manganese, potassium, selenium, zinc; omega-6 fatty acids; malic acid; tryptophan

RECIPE

1 mango, peeled, pitted and chopped into chunks
1¾ cups soymilk
1 tbsp. sunflower seeds

Whiz together the mango chunks and soymilk in a blender until smooth. Sprinkle the sunflower seeds over and drink immediately.

Because of its high iron content, mango is used in India to treat anemia.

carrot, nectarine & orange

Improve concentration with this bright-orange super-nutritious juice.

Brimful of antioxidant beta-carotene, this juice is also rich in folate, which has been found to help improve attention span and the ability to remember. Calcium and magnesium in the carrot and nectarine work together to relax nerve and muscle cells and to calm an "on-edge" feeling. The orange contains vitamin B5, needed to make the memory-sharpening neurotransmitter, acetylcholine.

NUTRIENTS
Vitamins B1, B3, B5, C, K, beta-carotene, folate; calcium, chromium, iron, magnesium, phosphorus, potassium; bioflavonoids

RECIPE

3 large carrots, topped, tailed, and chopped into chunks
2 nectarines, pitted and quartered
2 oranges, peeled and torn into segments

Press alternate chunks of carrot, nectarine and orange through a juicer, stir, and drink immediately.

apple, cucumber & peppermint

NUTRIENTS

Vitamins B1, B2, B3, C, K, beta-carotene, folate; calcium, iron, magnesium, manganese, phosphorus, potassium, selenium, silica, sodium, zinc; fructose; malic acid; pectin; tryptophan

This juice will perk up a fatigue-related mood dip.

About ten percent of an apple is made up of mood-stabilizing carbohydrates. The highly concentrated fructose in fresh apple juice revives energy slumps, which are a common cause of a low attention span. Cucumber is a valuable source of magnesium, a mineral that aids the formation of neurotransmitters in the brain. A rich source of zinc, which promotes mental alertness, peppermint also contains vitamin B1, which helps the body to turn the brain-fuel glucose into energy.

RECIPE

a handful fresh peppermint leaves
4 apples, cut into wedges
½ cucumber, chopped into chunks

Wrap the peppermint leaves around chunks of apple and cucumber. Press alternate chunks through a juicer, stir, and drink immediately.

broccoli, green bean, cabbage & sesame oil

A tasty treat full of brain-improving B-vitamins.

All three vegetables in this juice contain B-vitamins and are vital for good memory and concentration. Broccoli boasts a long list of nutrients, including zinc, which help to prevent depression, loss of appetite, lack of concentration, and that "blank-mind" feeling. Green beans provide the trace mineral manganese, needed for mood stability. The vitamin B6 found in cabbage aids in the formation of several brain neurotransmitters—crucial for good brain performance. The dash of sesame oil adds a distinct taste and beneficial omega-3 essential fatty acids.

NUTRIENTS
Vitamins B1, B2, B3, B5, B6, C, E, K; calcium, copper, iodine, iron, magnesium, manganese, phosphorus, potassium, zinc; omega-3 essential fatty acids; tryptophan

Red cabbage is known to have significantly more protective phytonutrients than white cabbage.

RECIPE

3 broccoli flowerets, chopped into chunks
½ medium cabbage, leaves separated and core chopped into chunks
25 green beans, topped and tailed
1 tsp. sesame oil

Press alternate chunks of broccoli and cabbage, and the green beans through a juicer. Stir in the sesame oil and drink immediately.

asparagus, beet & spinach

NUTRIENTS
Vitamins B1, B2, B3, B6, C, E, K, beta-carotene, biotin, folate; calcium, copper, iodine, iron, magnesium, manganese, phosphorus, potassium, zinc; tryptophan

This is brain food in liquid form to help the body's command center work at its best.

Even at rest the brain uses about 50 percent of the energy derived from food, and considerably more when active—for example, when we are reading. All three ingredients in this juice contain compounds that keep blood vessels supple and help to transport nerve impulses to the brain more efficiently.

Asparagus High in vitamin B6, which has been shown to decrease premenstrual mood swings and poor memory, just one serving of asparagus supplies almost 60 percent of the

Five spears of asparagus count as one portion of vegetables.

RECIPE

10½ oz. spinach leaves
10 asparagus spears, chopped into chunks
3 small beets, chopped into chunks
1 pinch cayenne pepper

Wrap the spinach leaves around chunks of asparagus and beets. Press alternate chunks through a juicer. Stir, sprinkle a little cayenne pepper over and drink immediately.

daily recommended intake of mood-stabilizing folate. It is also rich in all the B-vitamins that are necessary for relaxation.

Beet This vegetable is particularly rich in folate and magnesium, which are key to the production of the important brain chemical, dopamine. Low levels of dopamine are linked with an increased incidence of depression.

Spinach Thanks to its high iron content, spinach boosts the blood's ability to carry oxygen, increasing brain power, concentration, and memory. Spinach is also loaded with the antioxidants beta-carotene, vitamin C and folate.

Cayenne Pepper This spice increases blood circulation and helps to improve digestion.

PREPARATION TIPS

- Asparagus spears should be rounded with firm, thin stems and deep-green or purplish closed tips. Avoid those with fat, woody, or twisted stems.

- To keep asparagus fresh, place the bunch of spears, cut-side down, in 1 inch or so of water and store them in the refrigerator.

- Wash spinach leaves and stems thoroughly before juicing them, as they tend to collect sand and soil.

- To keep ground cayenne pepper fresh, store it in a tightly sealed glass jar away from direct sunlight.

097

carrot, leek & garlic

NUTRIENTS

Vitamins B1, B6, C, K, beta-carotene, folate; calcium, chromium, copper, iron, magnesium, manganese, phosphorus, potassium, selenium, sulfur; tryptophan

Help to balance brain chemicals and regulate hormone levels with this tasty, garlicky drink.

The beta-carotene in carrots is a potent antioxidant and has been shown to protect the brain from neurotoxins. The natural sulfur compounds in leeks help to reduce cholesterol and improve blood flow to the brain. Vitamin B6, found in leeks and garlic, aid the ability to remember and retrieve information, protecting against memory loss. B6 is also needed to make serotonin, melatonin, and dopamine—all important brain chemicals for hormone and mood balance.

To make this juice a bit less pungent, use garlic straight from the refrigerator.

RECIPE

4 large carrots, topped, tailed, and chopped into chunks
1 leek, topped, tailed, and chopped into chunks
2 cloves garlic, peeled

Press alternate chunks of carrot and leek, and the garlic, through a juicer, stir, and drink immediately.

yam, radish & parsley

The peppery radish cuts through the mild, starchy flavour of the yam for a perfectly balanced juice.

Yams are a good source of vitamin B6, essential for the absorption of fats and proteins, and manganese, which helps to metabolize carbohydrates and fuel the brain for prolonged periods. Traditionally used in eastern medicine for centuries, radishes contain substances that act in the same way as drugs used to treat degenerative brain conditions. The vitamin C in parsley juice helps to fight infections that make us feel low.

NUTRIENTS
Vitamins B1, B2, B3, B6, C, D, E, beta-carotene, folate; calcium, iodine, iron, magnesium, manganese, phosphorus, potassium, selenium, sulfur, zinc

RECIPE

1 medium white-flesh yam, peeled and chopped into chunks
20 radishes
1 handful fresh parsley sprigs

Press alternate chunks of yam, and the radishes and parsley sprigs through a juicer. Stir and drink immediately.

radish, lettuce & cucumber

NUTRIENTS
Vitamin C, beta-carotene, folate; calcium, iodine, iron, magnesium, manganese, phosphorus, potassium, silica, sulfur; tryptophan

Serve this juice over ice for a cooling mix that calms the mind and promotes positive thinking.

Rich in magnesium and calcium, radishes help to boost memory and concentration levels. Lettuce is 95 percent water, and the other five percent is a powerful cocktail of nutrients, which has been used to help beat insomnia and treat hyperactive children. Cucumber is a good source of tryptophan, an amino acid important in the production of serotonin—a brain chemical linked to positive mood.

Radishes contain the compound xylogen, which is known to help to destroy cancer cells.

RECIPE

½ head lettuce, separated into leaves
10 radishes, topped and tailed
1 cucumber, chopped into chunks

Wrap lettuce leaves around the radishes and chunks of cucumber. Press alternate ingredients through a juicer. Stir and drink immediately.

pepper, carrot & olive oil

This silky-smooth juice contains vitamins C and E, the brain-friendly duo shown to improve memory.

A high intake of vitamin C, found in bell pepper and carrot, can help reduce the symptoms of depression. Vitamin C also makes the vitamin E found in olive oil more effective, which helps to protect against free-radical damage. Both of these antioxidant vitamins have also been linked to better memory performance. The essential fatty acids in olive oil feed the brain's fatty tissues and this has a profound effect on positive thinking and well-being.

NUTRIENTS
Vitamins B1, B2, B6, C, D, E, K, beta-carotene, folate; calcium, chromium, copper, iron, magnesium, manganese, phosphorus, potassium; omega-3 and omega-6 fatty acids; tryptophan

RECIPE

2 bell peppers, seeded and chopped into chunks
4 large carrots, topped, tailed, and chopped into chunks
1 tbsp. olive oil

Press alternate chunks of bell pepper and carrot through a juicer. Stir in the olive oil and drink immediately.

ailments directory

ACNE

Acne is a skin disorder that is most common among teenagers, but also found in adults. Often triggered by hormonal factors, outbreaks occur when the skin's pores become clogged with sebum and dead cells. Topping up on vitamin A and E can help to ease this condition.

Juices to try

Watermelon, Peach & Pomegranate (p.25); Banana, Avocado & Soy Smoothie (p.58); Pepper, Carrot & Olive Oil (p.119)

ARTHRITIS (RHEUMATOID)

Rheumatoid arthritis is an inflammation of the joint tissues that leads to morning stiffness, pain, swelling, and redness. There is some evidence to support that antioxidant vitamins A and C, and selenium, can have a beneficial effect on arthritis.

Juices to try

Blackberry, Apple & Pineapple (p.38); Peach, Apricot & Mango (p.39); Carrot, Asparagus & Lemon Grass (p.78)

ASTHMA

Asthma is a condition in which the air tubes of the lungs contract in spasm, obstructing the flow of air and making breathing very difficult. Attacks are triggered by allergens, such as dust, pets, pollution, infections, emotional trauma, and physical activity. Boosting your antioxidant intake can help to reduce attacks and relieve symptoms.

Juices to try

Tofu & Raspberry Smoothie (p.56); Kiwi Fruit, Strawberry & Grape (p.94); Pepper, Tomato, Watercress & Olive Oil (p.104)

CANCER

This chronic disease, which can occur anywhere in the body, is characterized by an abnormal mass of cells that spreads. A diet high in antioxidants and phytochemicals can boost protection against cancer and also help to reverse the growth of tumors.

Juices to try
Beet, Grapefruit & Lime (p.15);
Berry & Yogurt Smoothie (p.98);
Carrot, Cauliflower & Turmeric
(p.102)

CANDIDIASIS

This is an infection caused
by the yeast, candida albicans,
often referred to as "thrush."
Medication (particularly
antibiotics, steroids, and
immunosuppressants),
stress, and poor diet can all
trigger the overgrowth of
candida. Vaginal thrush causes
abnormal discharge, irritation,
and soreness. You can restore
levels of good bacteria with
yogurt, and boost your
immunity with garlic.

Juices to try
Blackberry & Yogurt Smoothie
(p.27); Tomato, Celery, Garlic &
Basil (p.35); Watercress &
Yogurt Smoothie (p.37)

COMMON COLD

An infection of the upper
respiratory tract, a cold has
many symptoms including
sneezing, a stuffy or runny
nose, a sore throat, and feeling
under par. Effective remedies
include vitamin C, zinc, and
allicin (found in garlic), which
are all renowned for their
infection-fighting properties.

Juices to try
Grapefruit, Honey, Lemon
& Ginger (p.28); Orange, Kiwi
Fruit & Spinach (p.48); Carrot,
Leek & Garlic (p.116)

CYSTITIS

Usually occurring as a result
of infection, bruising, or
irritation, cystitis is an
inflammation of the urinary
tract. Symptoms include
frequent urination—often
with a burning sensation—
and a dragging pain in the
lower abdomen. Effective
remedies include cranberry
juice and wheat grass.

Juices to try
Cabbage, Carrot & Cranberry
(p.14); Squash, Brussels
Sprouts & Wheat Grass (p.47);
Cranberry, Yogurt & Goji Berry
Smoothie (p.71)

DEPRESSION (MILD)

A prolonged feeling of
unhappiness, which can be
overwhelming and lead to
feelings of hopelessness,
anxiety, and fear. Choosing
foods high in essential fatty
acids and B-vitamins can help
to reduce symptoms.

Juices to try

Avocado, Plum & Pear (p.45); Tofu, Blueberry & Hempseed Oil Smoothie (p.75); Broccoli, Green Bean, Cabbage & Sesame Oil (p.113)

ECZEMA

This inflammation of the skin causes itching, flakiness, redness, and scaly patches, which can form on and affect any part of the body. Common causes include food allergies and emotional stress. Try to relieve your symptoms by increasing your intake of vitamins A, B3, C and E.

Juices to try

Watercress & Yogurt Smoothie (p.37); Carrot, Cucumber, Olive & Basil (p.76); Black Currant, Banana & Yogurt Smoothie (p.85)

HAIR LOSS

It is normal to shed about 150 hairs a day, but increased stress, the aging process, and hormonal and hereditary factors can cause a faster rate of loss, resulting in thinning hair or baldness. Eating more foods containing zinc can help to stimulate hair growth.

Juices to try

Tofu & Raspberry Smoothie (p.56); Apple, Black Currant & Açai Berry (p.66); Pineapple, Orange & Coconut (p.73)

HAY FEVER

An allergic reaction to airborne irritants, such as grass, tree, or flower pollens, dust and animal fur, hay fever usually causes swelling of the nasal membrane. This stimulates the production of antibodies, which release histamine, the chemical substance that triggers the reaction. Vitamin C and the amino acid quercetin have been shown to ease the symptoms.

Juices to try

Tomato, Onion & Lemon (p.20); Blackberry, Apple & Pineapple (p.38); Avocado, Broccoli & Bok Choy (p.65); Apple, Cranberry & Plum (p.92)

HEART DISEASE

One of the main causes of heart disease is the blockage of arteries by cholesterol and waste matter. Avoid this by eating healthy monounsaturated oils, such as olive oil, and choosing high-fiber foods. Studies show that flavonoid plant compounds help lower cholesterol.

Juices to try

Tomato, Celery, Garlic & Basil (p.35); Avocado, Plum & Pear (p.45); Papaya, Apricot & Blueberry (p.81)

HERPES SIMPLEX

The virus that causes cold sores thrives on the amino acid arginine, found in chocolate and nuts, so avoid these foods. During an attack, foods rich in vitamin C and zinc can help to speed up the healing process.

Juices to try

Apple, Grape & Pomegranate (p.23); Watercress, Arugula & Tomato (p.36); Pepper, Onion, Garlic & Parsley (p.103)

INFERTILITY

The term "infertile" is generally applied to a couple who have not conceived after 18 months of trying. Eating zinc-rich foods and increasing your intake of vitamins B6 and E, and essential fatty acids is thought to boost fertility.

Juices to try

Pepper, Carrot, Lettuce & Alfalfa Sprout (p.51); Pepper, Tomato, Watercress & Olive Oil (p.104); Mango & Soymilk Smoothie (p.110)

INSOMNIA

Insomnia, or the disturbance of sleep patterns, can be caused by many factors, including emotional stress, pain, excess caffeine, food allergy, alcohol, and drugs. A combination of calcium and magnesium has been shown to regulate sleep patterns. The amino acid tryptophan triggers relaxation, encouraging sleep.

Juices to try

Avocado, Plum & Pear (p.45); Banana, Date, Apricot & Yogurt Smoothie (p.57); Zucchini, Lettuce & Parsley (p.63)

IRRITABLE BOWEL SYNDROME (IBS)

IBS is characterized by recurrent abdominal pain, and alternating diarrhea and constipation. It can also cause weight loss and poor nutrient absorption. To ease this condition, choose anti-inflammatory, antioxidant-rich foods, such as pineapple, strawberries, cherries, and sweet potatoes.

Juices to try

Carrot, Lemon & Flax Seed Oil (p.18); Strawberry, Cherry & Passion Fruit (p.68); Pineapple, Orange & Coconut (p.73)

MIGRAINE

A throbbing headache, often on only one side of the head, a migraine can be debilitating and last for up to two days. Avoiding potential trigger foods, such as caffeine, cheese, and red wine can help, as can increasing your intake of vitamins B5, C, and E.

Juices to try

Cucumber, Celery & Broccoli (p.19); Apple, Cherry & Blueberry (p.52); Asparagus, Beet & Spinach (p.114)

OBESITY

The excessive storage of energy in the form of fat, obesity is defined as a body weight of 20 percent more than the recommended maximum for a person's height. Drinking juices rich in the mineral chromium can help to stabilize blood sugar. Certain foods, including grapefruit, have fat-burning properties.

Juices to try

Grapefruit, Melon & Raspberry (p.26); Watercress & Yogurt Smoothie (p.37); Banana, Frozen Yogurt & Ginger Smoothie, (p.84); also see Weight Shifters (p22-37)

PREMENSTRUAL SYNDROME (PMS)

PMS describes a huge range of emotional, physical and behavioral symptoms that women experience in the week or two preceding menstruation. The cause is thought to be hormonal imbalance. Nutrients proven to help include evening primrose oil, magnesium, and vitamin B6.

Juices to try

Watermelon, Peach & Pomegranate (p.25); Apple, Carrot & Evening Primrose Oil (p.74); Avocado & Soy Yogurt Smoothie (p.79)

POLYCYSTIC OVARY SYNDROME (PCOS)

PCOS is a metabolic disorder that disrupts hormones, typically resulting in irregular periods, acne, excess body hair, and weight gain. Foods with a low glycemic load (GL) and essential fatty acids are believed to relieve the symptoms of this condition.

Juices to try

Apple, Carrot & Evening Primrose Oil (p.74); Tofu, Avocado & Soymilk Smoothie (p.105); Yam, Radish & Parsley (p.117)

glossary

VITAMINS

Vitamin A and Beta-carotene a fat-soluble vitamin that comes as retinol in animal produce and as carotenoids in plant foods; needed for healthy skin and eyes.

B1 (thiamin) involved in all key metabolic processes and useful for treating nervous disorders.

B2 (riboflavin) helps the body to convert sugar into energy and boosts skin, hair, and nail health.

B3 (niacin) helps to metabolize sugars, fats, and protein and maintain clear, healthy skin.

B5 (pantothenic acid) boosts energy and is involved in the formation of antibodies for a healthy immune response.

B6 (pyridoxine) needed for the production of antibodies and infection-fighting white blood cells.

B9 (folate) useful for heart health and in early pregnancy to help prevent the congenital defect, spina bifida.

B12 (cobalamin) essential for the healthy metabolism of nerve tissue; improves memory and concentration.

Biotin (vitamin H) helps to break down and metabolize fats; delays hair turning gray.

Vitamin C a water-soluble antioxidant that helps to neutralize harmful free radicals and boost immunity.

Vitamin D found in foods of animal origin and produced in the skin from the energy of the sun; good for bone health.

Vitamin E a fat-soluble antioxidant that helps to neutralize harmful free radicals, balance hormones, and ease skin conditions.

Vitamin K necessary for normal blood clotting and wound healing.

MINERALS

Calcium protects against osteoporosis, heart disease, and insomnia; useful in the treatment of heart disease.

Chromium helps to control sugar and cholesterol levels in the blood.

Copper protects against heart disease; important for the production of collagen in the skin.

Iodine determines healthy metabolism and helps to prevent thyroid disorders.

Iron encourages restful sleep and boosts energy levels and immunity.

Magnesium required for hormonal balance, energy production and cell replication.

Manganese necessary for the normal functioning of the brain and maintaining a healthy nervous system.

Phosphorus helps in formation of bones and teeth, and helps to fight fatigue.

Potassium activates enzymes that control energy production and maintains the water balance within cells.

Selenium stimulates the immune system and keeps eyes, skin, and hair healthy.

Silica helps bone development and promotes healthy skin, and connective tissues.

Silicon helps to prevent osteoporosis and to maintain the health of bones, skin, and nails.

Sulfur detoxifying; helps to treat digestive and skin disorders.

Zinc boosts the immune system and fertility levels; treats hair loss, skin disorders, and failing eyesight.

OTHERS
Acidophilus live, friendly bacteria found in some yogurts, which promote good digestion.

Allicin active ingredient in garlic and onions with antibacterial and antifungal properties.

Amino acids compounds, either made by the body or found in the diet, that are involved in processes such as the formation of neurotransmitters in the brain.

Anthocyanins dark purple antioxidant pigments found to aid blood flow.

Antioxidant prevents cell degeneration and decay.

Astringent constricts blood vessels or membranes in order to reduce irritation or swelling.

Betacyanin red pigment found in beets.

Bile fluid excreted by the liver that helps the body to digest fats.

Bromelain enzyme that assists protein digestion.

Carcinogen compound that can cause cancer.

Carotenoid yellow/orange pigment found in plants, including beta-carotene, which the body converts into vitamin A.

Chlorophyll green pigment found in plants, which has anti-carcinogenic properties.

Cholesterol waxy substance found in red blood cells.

Collagen protein essential for making ligaments, bones, teeth, and the "cement" that holds the skin together.

Coumarins chemicals with natural blood-thinning properties, which might help to prevent cancer.

Diuretic increases urine production.

Ellagic acid cancer-fighting substance found in berries.

Enzyme complex proteins that are produced by living cells, which trigger biochemical reactions.

Essential Fatty Acids (EFAs) fatty acids that are vital for healthy blood, skin, nerves, and the immune system.

Flavonoids anti-inflammatory antioxidants that work on the immune system.

Free radicals damaging molecules produced as a byproduct of metabolism or environmental factors.

Fructose simple sugar found in honey and fruits.

Gamma-linoleic Acid (GLA) omega-6 fatty acid important for immunity, healthy blood, skin, and nerves.

Glucose simple sugar.

Glycemic Index (GI) ranks foods according to their effect on blood sugar — foods with a high GI cause blood sugar to rise more quickly than low GI foods.

Glycemic Load (GL) ranks foods according to their effect on blood sugar and the quantity and quality of the carbohydrates.

Indoles plant compounds with anticancer properties.

Insulin hormone that regulates blood sugar levels.

Isoflavones compounds that mimic the action of the hormone oestrogen, helping to prevent hormone-related cancers.

Lactobacilli friendly bacteria that support the immune system, found in the gut. Obtained in the diet from milk products.

Lactose-intolerant the inability to digest lactose, the sugar naturally found in animal milk.

Laxative substance that triggers the evacuation of the bowels.

Limonin cancer-fighting chemical found in citrus fruit.

Lutein antioxidant carotenoid important for eye health.

Lycopene antioxidant carotenoid found in red pigments.

Malic acid helps the body to use energy efficiently.

Melatonin hormone shown to have antioxidant properties; helps to regulate sleep patterns.

Metabolism process in the body that converts food into energy.

Monounsaturated fat healthiest type of fat, which can help to lower cholesterol.

Papain enzyme found in papaya that aids protein digestion.

Pectin soluble fibre that helps to improve digestion and prevent heart disease.

Phytonutrient nutrient derived from a plant source.

Phytoestrogen plant compounds with effects similar, but weaker to, those of the hormone estrogen.

Polyphenols cancer-fighting chemical compounds found in plants.

Prostaglandins hormonelike substances that affect nervous, cardiovascular, gastrointestinal, urinary and endocrine systems.

Quercertin anti-inflammatory flavonoid found in onions.

Tannins astringent substances with antibacterial properties.

Volatile oils bio-active oils found in herbs and spices.

index

Author's acknowledgments
Thanks to my three boys – Harry, Jonah, and Luke – for their help and hugs. Huge thanks to my husband, Anthony, for his tea, love, and support.